THE
PARADOXICAL SELF

**Toward an Understanding of
Our Contradictory Nature**

THE PARADOXICAL SELF

Toward an Understanding of Our Contradictory Nature

Kirk J. Schneider, Ph.D.

Prefatory Note by
Rollo May

 INSIGHT BOOKS
PLENUM PRESS • NEW YORK AND LONDON

Library of Congress Cataloging-in-Publication Data

Schneider, Kirk J.
    The paradoxical self : toward an understanding of our
contradictory nature / Kirk J. Schneider.
        p.   cm.
    Includes bibliographical references.
    ISBN 0-306-43268-4
    1. Paradox. 2. Self. 3. Psychology, Pathological.   I. Title.
RC455.4.P35S34 1989
    155.2--dc20   89-38660
                                                                 CIP

© 1990 Kirk J. Schneider
Plenum Press is a Division of
Plenum Publishing Corporation
233 Spring Street, New York, N.Y. 10013
An Insight Book

Printed in the United States of America

TO MY PARENTS
AND TO THE MEMORY OF
DR. MURRAY H. SCHNEIDER,
WHOSE IMPACT ON A FEW
HAS MEANT SO MUCH

PREFATORY NOTE

The distinguishing virtue of Kirk Schneider's book is that the author refuses both the emptiness of shallow optimism and the hangdog attitude of pessimism. He does this by means of the paradox.

This is the paradox of life about which Paul Tillich, Kierkegaard, Nietzsche, and others talk, but which in our age of pseudoprosperity has been forgotten. Schneider argues that genuine joy of life and creativity come out of this polarity. He values the paradox which profound thinkers have always pointed out. He has great company consisting of Kierkegaard, Tillich, Ernest Becker, and many others down through history.

Though this is not the kind of book which Kierkegaard describes as good for "perusing during one's afternoon nap," it is a book which calls us back to the fundamentals of life and psychology. It reminds one of the phrase Tillich believed was fundamental, namely "living in spite of." *The Paradoxical Self* will especially help psychology to get back to its great calling again.

ROLLO MAY

PREFACE

For what does the great spirit need that touches the body but the touch of the body, as oratory needs silence, and revolution peace? We are nourished by our absences and opposites; contraries quench our thirst.

—William H. Gass

Contraries, contradictions, paradoxes. We are steeped in them. Yet so many of us deny their power. We are "nourished by our opposites" and yet we continue to smooth them over or push them aside. We continue to live our lives simplistically—within little personal, cultural, or vocational niches; or we live them excessively—as warriors, thrill-seekers, zealots, bullies, pedants, and pawns. We have to "line-up," "straighten out," "cut loose." We have to be "for" or "against," "friend" or "foe," "all or none." Our world splinters because of these polarities. Minds shatter. It is not enough to say that such denial prompts human beings to kill. Insanity, prejudice, oppression—every kind of social and emotional "rape" stems from this avoidance.

And yet even the smallest gesture toward *affirming* paradox (contradiction, contrast) in our lives would alleviate many of these ills. The problem, however, is that too many of us are afraid, even horrified by such a prospect. On the surface of it, this simply does not make sense. Why would so many be repelled by the

very instrument of their salvation? Why would generations upon generations continue to forsake it?

These are exactly the questions I posed for myself
in this book. Just what is this paradox that causes so
much suffering—and yet such promise and exaltation?
How can we face it, begin to get a grip on it, bring it into
our lives?

This book, accordingly, is for students, profession-
als, and lay readers who struggle with similar questions,
and the challenges they so urgently pose.

KIRK J. SCHNEIDER

Newton, Massachusetts

ACKNOWLEDGMENTS

This book owes its origins to many late-night discussions. My deepest appreciation goes to J.A. Bricker who made these discussions possible—challenging, debating, supporting.

Much appreciation to John Galvin, Ilene Serlin, Don Cooper, Stanley Krippner, Gerald Stechler, and Linda Conti who were kind enough to read the manuscript through at the first draft stage and provide invaluable feedback.

I am indebted to Saybrook Institute and West Georgia College for their humanity and rigor. In addition to those already mentioned, I would also like to thank Jim and Elizabeth Bugental, Don Rice, and Bob Masek.

I am particularly indebted to Rollo May, who is in great part the inspiration for this endeavor.

My sincerest gratitude, finally, to Jurate Raulinaitis for her editing and wonderful companionship.

Grateful acknowledgment is made for permission to quote from the following sources:

J. van den Berg, *A different existence: Principles of phenomenological psychopathology*. Pittsburgh: Duquesne University Press. Copyright © 1972 by Duquesne University.

L. Binswanger, The case of Ellen West. (W. Mendel & J. Lyons, Trans.). In R. May, E. Angel, & H. Ellenberger (Eds.), *Existence: A new dimension in psychi-*

CONTENTS

13

INTRODUCTION

Only the paradox comes anywhere near to comprehending the fullness of life.

—C.G. Jung

There is a concept which corrupts and upsets all the others. I refer not to Evil, whose limited realm is that of ethics, I refer to the infinite.

—Jorge Luis Borges

Why do so many of us become extreme? Why do some of us *isolate* ourselves from society, or *shrink* at the first opportunity to meet another person, or *nitpick* at minute details? By contrast, why do some of us *indulge* in relationships, *seethe* with hostility, or *overflow* with desires?

Why do many of us become conformists? What makes us live out our extremes through the actions of others—institutions, ideologies, heros; or things—fashions, drugs, machines? What prompts us to commit the most abhorrent acts, such as war, in the name of these devotions?

Finally, why do a few of us confront and optimally *transform* our extremes? What spurs some of us to achieve vital relationships, personally and socially meaningful careers, and revolutionary creations?

19

These questions are among the most complex and pressing of our time. Yet the proposed answers to them seem increasingly pale to many of us. Either they address our genes but forget our minds or they address our minds but forgo our genes. Or they address both but deny our hearts and the other way around. Either we are free, they declare, or we are determined; perfect or perfectly hopeless. We are drowning in a sea of half-views!

On the pages to follow, accordingly, I will examine an alternative that has not been permitted enough of a "voice." It is a view that derives mainly from existential psychology, but it is surely in part my own creation.

Before too many readers are "scared off" by that term "existential," let me assure you that I, too, have difficulty with allegedly helpful, but for all practical purposes, impenetrable ideas. The model I am about to present, therefore, is as clear, concrete, and relevant as I can render it.[1]

---

[1]Although some existentialists fear that unifying and systematizing their approach might lead to the very dogmatism they have fought to overcome (e.g., see Sartre, 1957), I am not of this opinion. The very purpose of existentialism is to extract common, sharable *themes* about living, not universal laws (van Kaam, 1966). By definition, this process avoids dogmatism, and demands periodic refinements. Moreover, I share a growing body of opinion (e.g., Faulconer & Williams, 1985; Giorgi, 1987; Maslow, 1971; O'Hara, 1985; Rogers, 1985) that if the existential understanding is to have a lasting impact on society, it must be brought down from its tower and applied to society. The field is simply too germane today to be passed over as "obscure."

PARADOX AND THE LONG SHADOW OF KIERKEGAARD

Over a century ago, a brilliant but little known essay inaugurated modern existential psychology: "Despair Viewed Under the Aspects of Finitude and Infinitude." This masterwork, by Søren Kierkegaard (1954, p. 162), is a sweeping analysis of human character, and anticipates the model of existential psychology that we present here. Kierkegaard's aim was to describe human capabilities and limits, or, in other words, consciousness. His essential thesis was that consciousness is paradoxical.[2] "The self is a synthesis [of two factors]," he writes, "one of which is constantly opposed to the other" (Kierkegaard, 1954, p. 163). People's experiences, he elaborates, tend to fall between two potentially endless extremes—the "finitized" and the "infinitized." Finitized experience is characterized by restriction and submission. Infinitized experience is characterized by mobility and domination.

Kierkegaard then went on to suggest that finitized and infinitized capacities take on a great variety of meanings for people as they develop. For example, the admonition to "shut up" can feel stifling to a child who is verbally expressive (i.e., infinitized). Likewise, isolation, tranquility, and order, essentially finitized experiences, may associate with suffocation for a person who craves a great deal of stimulation. Finally, finitized clas-

---

[2] By "paradoxical" I mean "having"—and potentially reconciling— "contradictory qualities" (*Webster's New World Dictionary*, 1968, p. 1060).

sification, organization, and conformity may feel oppressive to a more free-wheeling type.

The net effect of such frightful associations, Kierkegaard indicates, is an *increase* in the opposite behavior (in this case "infinitizing" behavior). The net effect of that occurrence, he goes on, is dysfunction or what he terms the "fantastical" (Kierkegaard, 1954, p. 164). "Generally," Kierkegaard (1954) explains,

> the fantastical is that which so carries a [person] out into the infinite that it merely carries him away from himself and therewith prevents him from returning to himself.

By contrast, there are many people for whom finitizing (restricting and submitting) behavior is comfortable and infinitizing (mobilizing and dominating) behavior is frightening. Such people, for example, associate assertiveness, curiosity, and experimentation with a great deal of dread. In turn, they become more finitized—quieter, more reserved, and more rigid to counteract this anxiety. Kierkegaard (1954) elaborates:

> The despair of finitude is due to the lack of infinitude. . . . [Hence] while one sort of despair plunges wildly into the infinite and loses itself, a second sort permits itself as it were to be defrauded. (p.166)

A person in such a condition, Kierkegaard (1954) continues,

> forgets himself, forgets what his name is, . . . does not dare to believe in himself, finds it too venturesome a thing to be himself, far easier and safer to be like the others, to become an imitation, a number, a cipher in a crowd. (pp. 166–167)

On the other hand, Kierkegaard (1954) found that finitized and infinitized modes of expression are not always intimidating to people. Healthier people, he showed, are enlivened (at least to a point) by these modes. Such people learn to associate adaptation, rather than threat, with restrictive, submissive, mobile, or dominant actions. The person who achieves selfhood (health), Kierkegaard (1954) explains, achieves a finitized/infinitized "synthesis" (p. 162). The person who succumbs to dysfunction becomes a fragment of a self—either overly finitized to escape infinitized associations, or overly infinitized to escape finitized associations. Elsewhere he concludes: "Health consists essentially in being able to resolve contradictions. . . . The condition of [one's] survival is therefore analagous to breathing (respiration), which is an in- and an a-spiration" (Kierkegaard, p. 173).

Despite the power of this analysis, Kierkegaard's language makes it very difficult for people to understand and apply his work. "Infinitize," for example, is intended to convey "expansiveness," not literally boundlessness. One *approaches* boundless thoughts, feelings, and sensations, Kierkegaard implies; one probably does not literally experience them. Similarly, Kierkegaard's "finitize" is intended to convey "constriction," not literally the annihilation of experience. Hence, one *approaches* annihilation of thoughts, feelings, and sensations; one does not literally perceive this. In short, constriction and expansion are better suited, in my opinion, for the continuous (as opposed to misleading dichotomous) nature of Kierkegaard's psychology.

The second problem with Kierkegaard's dualities is their degree of abstraction. We need to know more about how people *experience* finitizing and infinitizing—how they are felt, sensed, and expressed intellectually.

Given these problems, let me now present a reformulation of Kierkegaard's thesis. I call it the "paradox principle." The paradox principle, as we shall see, is rooted not only in Kierkegaard's writings, but in the writings of numerous other existential theorists.[3]

In the balance of this book, I will first explain the basic assumptions of the paradox principle, and then apply them to dysfunctional, conventional, optimal, and therapeutic psychological domains.[4]

[3]The paradox principle is based on existential-phenomenological rather than purely existential or phenomenological traditions in psychology. The paradox principle thus draws from both phenomenological observations, which emphasize the unique perspective of the individual, and existential writings, which emphasize the sharable or intersubjective viewpoints that are built upon the phenomenological data (Giorgi, 1970; Merleau-Ponty, 1962).

Existential-phenomenological psychology, it should be further noted, differs from both Sartrian existential psychology and Husserlian phenomenological psychology. Existential-phenomenological psychology stresses *both* humanity's reflective (i.e., purposeful, aware) *and* prereflective (uncertain, limited) qualities. The Sartrian and Husserlian views, on the other hand, stress only humanity's reflective aspect. See May (1958a, 1958b), Merleau-Ponty (1962), and Spiegelberg (1976) for a fuller discussion of these issues.

Finally, the theme of paradox, it must be recognized, has a prominent philosophical and literary heritage. Among the contributors are Greek philosophers Zeno, Heraclitus, and Socrates; Chinese thinker Lao Tzu; writers William Blake, William Shakespeare, and Johann von Goethe; and 19th-century philosophers Georg Hegel, Søren Kierkegaard, and Friedrich Nietzsche.

[4]Terms such as "psyche," "psychological," "experience," "consciousness," "behavior," and "perception" are used throughout this book in the existential-phenomenological sense, unless otherwise indicated. Existential-phenomenology views all references to mind and body as a gestalt (e.g., in terms of "figure/ground"). For example, one cannot definitively separate emotional experience from sense-perception (Merleau-Ponty, 1962).

Chapter One

THE PARADOX PRINCIPLE: BASIC ASSUMPTIONS

It's got to have paradox, it's got to have contradiction, it's got to have conflict, or it isn't a powerful human feeling.
—Philosopher Phillip Hallie

The paradox principle embraces the following basic assumptions: (1) The human psyche is a constrictive/expansive continuum, only degrees of which are conscious. (2) *Dread* of constrictive or expansive polarities promotes dysfunction, extremism, or polarization (the degree and frequency of which is generally proportionate to the degree and frequency of one's dread). (3) *Confrontation* with or integration of the poles promotes optimal living.[1]

[1]It is important to note that so-called optimal living is more likely to be a "state" rather than a "trait." People achieve *moments* of synthesis or integration of the poles, not usually lifetimes (Becker, 1973; Riegel, 1976). The criterion for being "integrated," as we shall see, is intimately connected with one's courage. Can one *affirm*

Let us look more closely now at the first of these assumptions. The latter two will be taken up in detail in subsequent chapters.

The human psyche shifts between two poles (or modes) which are potentially endless in scope: the constrictive and the expansive. The constrictive pole is defined as the perceived "drawing back" and confinement of thoughts, feelings, and sensations. The expansive pole is the perceived "bursting forth" and extension of thoughts, feelings, and sensations (see Binswanger, 1975; Prentky, 1979). These poles are characterized by a variety of words and mannerisms. Constriction, for example, may be experienced in terms of retreating, diminishing, refining, falling, emptying, or slowing. Expansion may be viewed as gaining, enlarging, dispersing, ascending, filling, or accelerating.

---

one's polarities (e.g., selfishness/communalism; cooperativeness/competitiveness; tenderness/toughness; formality/informality) in given situations, or does one retreat from them? Although I believe that everyone retreats from the polarities to some degree, the question is how much and in what context? The final arbiter of this issue is oneself, or, to the extent one affects others, the "marketplace of ideas." The question is, how *convincing* is one's deed to oneself and others; not how "true" is it. Although existentialists cannot tell people where and in what degree they can convincingly affirm paradox, they can alert them to the general profundity of such an affirmation. They can provide a fruitful direction, based on strong empirical evidence, for humanity to strive.

The phrase "integration of paradox," it should be further noted, is not intended to convey "transcendence" or "elimination" of paradox. It is not intended to convey the attainment of "harmony," "wholeness," or "perfect balance." On the contrary, "integration" is intended to be a dynamic, unfinished engagement, always limited to a context. I will have more to say on both of the above points in Chapter Five.

Constriction and expansion represent two basic stances toward space and time (universal human dimensions according to existentialists—see Ellenberger, 1958)[2]: perception through exclusion and inclusion. When one excludes the emphasis is on reducing, blocking out, and narrowing. The experience of yielding, for

[2]Space and time, according to existentialists, underlie three basic modes of human existence—the *umwelt* or biological, the *eigenwelt* or subjective, and the *mitwelt* or interpersonal (May, 1958b; Ellenberger, 1958). Although the extension of our bodies and minds through space and time is fairly self-evident, the latter mode may require further elaboration. Accordingly, our relations with others take place within the spatial dimension as follows: "I live *near* the one I love"; "I am *distant* from those I dislike"; I *extend* myself to others when I feel sociable"; "I *withdraw* when I feel shy."

Interpersonal relations take place within the temporal as these experiences amplify: "I commune with my *ancestry*"; "I work for *future* generations"; "I feel very *present* to this person."

It should be further noted that when existentialists speak of space and time, they are not referring merely to physical but cognitive and emotional dimensions as well (Ellenberger, 1958). Language, the apparent basis of cognition, for example, operates within space and time. Verbs or action words convey dynamic movement—"go," "stay," "fly." Nouns and pronouns separate and delimit spatial areas—"I," "he," "Joe," "tree," "it," "we," "they." Articles—"the," and coordinating conjunctions, "and," "but,"—also direct and specify spaces and times. Adjectives—"beautiful," "ugly," "careworn" etc.—circumscribe spaces and times that often have an emotional charge to them. Tenses delimit time—"went," "stayed," "flew," "could," "may," "will." Punctuation, finally, serves as the "traffic manager" of language.

Emotions also appear to be delimited by space and time, although they are, perhaps, more difficult to understand in this context. Anger, for example, is often experienced in terms of large spaces and short bursts of time. Sadness tends to be perceived in terms of small spaces and sluggish temporal dimensions. Other emotions, as we shall see, are descriptive on a similar basis.

example, is primarily an exclusion of *one's own* space and time. Instances of yielding are conforming to others' political views, assuming others' emotional burdens, or giving in to others' physical will.

Focusing is another primarily exclusive experience. When one focuses one excludes aspects of *one's own and others'* (including inanimate others') space-time. Some examples are reducing a smile to a physiochemical process, attending to a single emotion, monitoring the beat of one's heart.

When one includes, on the other hand, one adds to, links together, and enlarges one's experiential field. The experience of asserting, for example, is an inclusion, primarily, of *one's own* space and time. This is illustrated by creating, directing, and subduing.

The experience of incorporating, likewise, is an inclusion of *one's own and others'* space and time. This is exemplified by exploring ideas, supporting a friend, or rescuing a swimmer.

These constrictive and expansive poles are perceived in degrees and probably cannot be *totally* embraced (see Heelas & Lock, 1981; Riegel, 1976; Schneider, 1987). For example, Brown (1977) showed that meditators can achieve profound degrees of constrictive and expansive awareness. However, notable evidence (e.g., Becker, 1973, 1975; Bharati, 1976; Brown, 1977; Pahnke & Richards, 1972) also indicates that such people probably cannot span the entire continuum. Prentky (1979) makes a similar claim about creative geniuses. "Too much deviation," he wrote,

> in the form of extreme abstraction or concretization, predisposes the individual to psychiatric disorder. . . . As mental illness begins to intrude, creativity recedes into the background (p. 33).

Sadler (1969), finally, viewed intuition as a kind of felt thought which can move only partially beyond personal space and time—the boundaries of our bodies, cultures, and values.

The determination as to which mode—constriction or expansion—manifests in a situation is made primarily by the perceiver. The perceiver can usually disclose—through words, symbols, or actions—his or her sense of confinement or extension. Contrary to the "arousal" thesis put forth by positivists (e.g., Eysenck, 1957), the modes cannot be discerned by strict physiological means. For example, one's sense of constriction may or may not conform to an "objective" reading of the parasympathetic nervous system; the same can be said about expansion and sympathetic action. The best way to find out which mode people perceive is by asking them and empathically listening to them.[3]

Reflection is defined as the extent to which people are aware of their constrictive and expansive potentialities. Prereflection refers to the extent to which people are unaware of those potentialities (i.e., as in the case of constrictive or expansive dream material). Psychical functioning, in other words, is viewed here in modified Freudian terms. We can constrict and expand only so far; the rest is latent, obscure, unreachable (see also Kant, 1929).

What I term one's centric mode (from now on called simply "centric" or "center") is a broadened ver-

---

[3]Although most of the data included in this book are phenomenological in nature (i.e., from the point of view of the relevant subject), several studies are researcher- or observer-based. The latter, however, are not intended to displace the phenomenological data, but to build upon and articulate it.

sion of Freud's "ego" The centric, like the ego, is the directive core of consciousness but its power does not derive only from sense perception or social-parental influences (internalizations). Affective, intuitive, and imaginative capacities may also temper centric functioning. Furthermore, the aim of the centric, like the ego, is to control psychic forces, but not always in a dominating fashion. It does not always attempt to subdue sexual and aggressive urges. It attempts to control, that is, engage, all of one's capabilities to the degree (personal, social, environmental, and cosmic) circumstances permit one.

Specifically, the centric refers to one's capacity (courage) to be aware of and direct one's constrictive and expansive potentialities. Generally, the more one is aware of context (i.e., psychophysiological, social, historical, and prospective), the stronger one's centric. The less one is aware of context, the weaker one's centric.

Lifton's (1976) concept of "centering" is similar. "Centering," Lifton explains, is "the ordering of experience by the self along the various dimensions that must be dealt with at any given moment—temporal, spatial, and emotional" (p. 71).

Bugental (1978, pp. 84–90) views centering as the quality of one's "presence" to thoughts, feelings, or actions. "Again and again," he writes,

> I am astonished to recognize how people who have clearly demonstrated their effectiveness in the external world still live in such cramped fashion within their own souls and still have such anguish and frustration in trying to explore within their own lives.

> What I want to describe is a way of being in our own centers in which we are open to inward awareness so that we can explore within our consciousness, discover

fresh conceptions, evolve different ways of seeing familiar circumstances, and extend the range of our personal possibilities. (Bugental, 1978, pp. 84–85)

May (1969), finally, voices a related understanding with his concept of intentionality:

Intentionality is what underlies both conscious and unconscious intentions. It refers to a state of being and involves, to a greater or lesser degree, the *totality* of the person's orientation to the world at that time. (p. 252)

To sum up then, the centric is one's presence in or involvement with one's constrictive and expansive potentialities. It is the range in which—given one's concrete limitations—one is capable of yielding, focusing, asserting, or incorporating.

Summarizing the paradox principle's basic assumptions: The psyche is a constrictive/expansive continuum, only degrees of which are conscious. Constriction is defined as the perceived "drawing back" and confinement of thoughts, feelings, and sensations; expansion is understood as the perceived "bursting forth" and extension of thoughts, feelings, and sensations. Constrictive consciousness is characterized by yielding and focusing elements; expansive consciousness is marked by asserting and incorporating elements.

What I term one's "centric mode" or "center" is the capacity to be aware of and direct one's constrictive and expansive potentialities.

Dread of constrictive or expansive polarities promotes dysfunction, extremism, or polarization; appropriate *confrontation* with or integration of the poles promotes optimal living.

Now let us explore *dysfunctional* experiences. How do sufferers describe them? What are their ranges? Why are they of such interest?

Chapter Two

DYSFUNCTIONAL EXTREMES

Madness fascinates because it is knowledge.

—Michel Foucault

If there is a gleaming pearl in the work of Michel Foucault (1965), it is his intriguing claim that madness delimits sanity. The extremes of constrictive and expansive awareness, as Kierkegaard, too, had shown, inform us not only about what is destructive in human potentiality but also what is inventive, visionary, and far-sighted. Psychopathy, narcissism, obsessions, and the like are not only blights to be avoided, they are treasures to be harnessed.

While this theory may seem overly sentimental, phenomenological research, in my opinion, points to no other reasonable conclusion. There are four relevant data here: many highly creative people become dysfunctional; some dysfunctional people become creative;

dysfunctional extremes appear to delimit functional extremes, and not the other way around; and dysfunctional people appear to experience more spatiotemporal alterations for more continuous clock hours than even our most transcendent citizenry (Arieti, 1976; Becker, 1973; Holden, 1987; Laing, 1967; Lombroso, 1910; Pahnke & Richards, 1972; Prentky, 1979; Sass, 1987; Vonnegut, 1975).

For these reasons, then, I will now describe the vicissitudes of the mad. This portrayal is not meant to be exhaustive or formally diagnostic. It is meant to be suggestive, to set the stage for further empirical and theoretical work, as well as upcoming sections of this book. I have drawn here from both my own and others' (phenomenological) observations.

DESCRIPTIONS OF THE DYSFUNCTIONAL

What follows is the paradox principle's understanding of extreme or "hyper" constriction and expansion. I use this terminology because I have found it more useful than the neurosis/psychosis distinction to understand both the continuity and structure of dysfunctional action.

There are three essential points to bear in mind about hyperconstriction and hyperexpansion (which can be preceded by "mild," "moderate," and "severe" if diagnostically useful). First, they are rarely unidimensional. Constriction and expansion almost invariably intrude upon one another to some degree. Partly this is due to their continuous nature (i.e., expansion implies some degree of constriction and vice versa). Sometimes, however, this is due to what Freud and Jung (1958) called "the return of the repressed" phenomenon. This phenomenon conveys, essentially, that no single way of experiencing can be fixated upon indefinitely; contradictory elements invariably arise.

One of the best illustrations of this concept is provided by Freud (1963). "Slips of the tongue," "slips of the pen," and "accidents" are all striking exemplars of return of the repressed. Such occurrences are inopportune, and appear to serve "unconscious" motives. Specifically, they appear to liberate (that is, bring to conscious awareness) repressed sexual or aggressive wishes (Freud, 1963). A man who is unconsciously attracted to a woman, for example, might make an unintended sexual remark, or stumble in her presence. Conversely, a woman who is unconsciously hostile toward her husband might forget her married name.

From the standpoint of the paradox principle, these "slips" are understood on "constrictive" and "expansive" grounds. For example, sexuality and aggression are viewed in the wider context of expanding ("bursting forth" and "extending"). One can expand in numerous ways—by creating, imagining, aspiring, affiliating, and trusting as well as seducing and aggressing. The more one represses this expansiveness (just as with sexuality), the more one is likely to experience its return. For example, a man who chronically suppresses his imagination will probably daydream at undesirable times. A woman who repeatedly denies her need to affiliate will probably compound that need at an inadvisable moment.

Similar cases can be made for the denial of one's constrictive potentialities—obligations, duties, priorities—all the ways that one "draws back" and confines. For example, a boy who continually spurns self-

discipline will increase the likelihood that someone else
will discipline him. A girl who continually dodges her
job duties will increase the likelihood of feeling burdened by those duties. The upshot of these scenarios is
that the return of the repressed phenomenon is operational on many constrictive and expansive fronts; sexuality and aggression are just two of them.

The second point to bear in mind about constrictive
and expansive extremes is that they are *relative*. There is
no absolute extremity; only the judgments of those concerned (e.g., clients) or those able to articulate the perspective of those concerned (e.g., empathic observers).

Finally, dysfunctional extremes are characterized
by a "forced" or "compulsive" quality. One tends to feel
"taken over" by them, rather than "centered in" or relatively controlling of them. For example, "healthier"
people engage in exploratory behavior *primarily* out of a
sense of *interest*. They exercise a certain degree of *choice*
in the matter. Manic people, on the other hand, engage
in exploratory behavior *primarily* out of a sense of panic.
They feel they *must* engage such behavior.

Now let us look more closely at a variety of dysfunctional syndromes.

HYPERCONSTRICTION

Depression has been described by various investigators as perhaps the ultimate collapse of one's experiential world (Becker, 1973; Binswanger, 1975). Depression is marked by profound slowness, isolation,
oppression, and impotency. One's world literally closes
and darkens (van den Berg, 1972). Sartre (1948a) puts it
this way:

Sadness is characterized by . . . a behavior of oppression; there is muscular resolution, pallor, coldness at the extremities; one turns toward a corner and remains seated, motionless, offering the least possible surface to the world. One prefers shade to broad daylight, silence to noise, the solitude of a room to crowds in public places. (p. 64)

Elsewhere he comments: "Sadness aims to eliminate the obligation to seek new ways . . . to transform the structure of the world" (Sartre, 1948a, p. 65).

Binswanger (1958a, p. 194) characterizes depression as a "shrinking" and "narrowing" of one's "world-design." Becker (1973) puts it similarly:

Depressive psychosis is the extreme on the continuum of *too much necessity*, that is, too much finitude, too much limitation by the body . . . [It is] a bogging down in the demands of others—family, job, the narrow horizons of daily duties. In such a bogging down the individual does not feel or see that he has alternatives.

Obsessive-compulsiveness, a perhaps less severe constrictive dysfunction, is marked by extreme focalizing and ritualizing. Von Gebsattel (1958) summed the obsessive-compulsive profile this way:

Its characteristics are narrowness, natureless monotony, and rigid, rule-ridden unchangeability—all of which are most essential alterations of the mode of moral, spatial, and temporal being-in-the-world. (p. 185)

Becker (1973) elaborates:

Here we see the result of too much fetishization or partialization, too much narrowing-down of the world for action. The result is that the person gets stuck in the narrowness. It is one thing to ritually wash one's hands three times; it is another to wash them until the hands bleed and one is in the bathroom most of the day. (p. 180)

Finally, Shapiro (1965) concretizes these remarks:

> The most conspicuous characteristic of the obsessive-compulsive's attention is its intense, sharp focus. These people are not vague in their attention. They concentrate, and particularly do they concentrate on detail. This is evident, for example, in the Rorschach test in their accumulation, frequently, of large numbers of small "detail responses" and their precise delineation of them . . . and the same affinity is easily observed in daily life. Thus, these people are very often found among technicians; they are interested in, and at home with, technical details. (p. 27)

From the standpoint of the paradox principle, the obsessive-compulsive fears the penetration of expansion—novelty, fluidity, uncertainty—into his or her world. "Every interval of passing time, then, is experienced as a threat of increasing the possible losses of form in the chained person and deepens the worry . . . about [his or her] ability to be" (von Gebsattel, 1958, p. 187).

Whereas the above syndromes are highlighted by emotional and cognitive factors, social factors mark the overly dependent. Dependent people avoid interpersonal risk. They subordinate their needs to others, and are greatly plagued by guilt (Millon, 1981):

> Dependent personalities tend to denigrate themselves and their accomplishments. What little self-esteem they possess is determined largely by the support and encouragement of others. . . . Losing the affection and protection of those upon whom they depend leads them to feel exposed to the void of self-determination. To

protect themselves, dependents quickly submit and comply with what others wish, or make themselves so pleasing that no one could possibly ignore them. (p. 107)

Dependency, then, is an overreliance on people. Autonomy is perceived as beyond one's pale—physically, emotionally, or intellectually.

Anxiety (and I speak here of "anxiety disorder" as opposed to the "dread" that precedes every defensive reaction) is a related dysfunction. Anxiety entails a constriction of one's capabilities (especially those "central" to one's identity). Whereas dependency, like depression, implies resignation from those capabilities, anxiety implies some degree of struggle. One is afraid but one has not given up the fight to reclaim one's life. One is often tense, hypervigilant, and apprehensive, but not, as yet, immobile. Anxiety is contrasted from fear, finally, in that it is subjective, without an objective referent. May (1977) elaborates:

Neurotic anxiety . . . is that which occurs when the incapacity for coping adequately with threats is not objective but subjective—i.e., is due not to objective weakness but to inner psychological patterns and conflicts which prevent the individual from using his powers. (p. 189)

"The more creative the individual," May (1977) concludes, "the more possibilities he or she has and the more [he or she is] confronted with anxiety" (p. 356).

Psychotic anxiety, on the other hand, or what Laing (1969) terms "petrification," is probably the most devastating assessment of one's powers. Whereas the anxiety neurotic anticipates helplessness, the psychotic expects annihilation. "Petrification," writes Laing

(1969), is "a particular form of terror, whereby one is petrified, turned to stone." It is also

> the dread of this happening: the dread, that is, of the possibility of turning, or being turned, from a live person into a dead thing, into a stone, into a robot, an automaton, without personal autonomy of action, an *it* without subjectivity. (p. 46)

Anxiety, then, is the suffocating fear, not of an object, but of the collapse of one's potentialities, perhaps even life. This suffocation is wide-ranging, from crippling autonomic reactions to immobilizing terror.

In fears and phobias, which pertain more to a specific object or area of concern, time and space are similarly warped. People or objects in the phobic's world accrue awesome proportions. They are large, powerful, explosive, or persecutory. They force the fearful one into emotional or physical corners. They impinge upon his or her specific desires or needs. One "can't" go to the store because a snake may lie in wait. One shrinks from crowds because crippling embarassment may ensue. One cannot befriend a person of another race lest one will be cursed or hexed or contaminated.

Van den Berg (1972) describes a phobic patient of his who observed the street from his house:

> The houses . . . gave the impression of being closed up, as if all the windows were shuttered, although he could see this was not so. He had an impression of closed citadels. And, looking up, he saw the houses leaning over toward the street, so that the strip of sky between the roofs was narrower than the street on which he walked. On the square, he was struck by an expanse that far exceeded the width of the square. He knew for certain that he would not be able to cross it. An attempt

to do so would, he felt, end in so extensive a realization of emptiness, width, rareness and abandonment that his legs would fail him. He would collapse. . . . It was the expanse, above all, that frightened him. (p. 9)

Binswanger (1958a) elucidates the time-disturbance experienced by the phobic individual:

We must not forget that where the world-design is naı-rowed and constricted to such a degree, the self too ıs constricted and prevented from maturing. Everything is supposed to stay as it was before. If, however, something new does happen and continuity is disrupted, it can only result in catastrophe, panic, anxiety attack. For then the world actually collapses, and nothing is left to hold it up. . . . The world must stop here, nothing must happen, nothing must change. (p. 204)

Arcaya (1979) elaborates:

Time contracts as the future and past are ignored in favor of the immediately perceived situation. As the threatening object nears . . . space . . . is no longer perceived as an area with multiple possibilities. Instead, it is delimited and constricted. The fearsome object encroaches upon [one's] lived space, leaving [one] with few if no personal boundaries. (p. 175)

The notion that one must resist venturing out and that the world is a hostile, brutalizing force is brought dramatically to the fore by so-called paranoid states. Whereas phobics tend to focus their concerns on objects and events, paranoiacs focus on people. Cameron (1963) elaborates:

The paranoid personality is one that has its origin in a lack of basic trust. . . . Because of his basic lack of trust in others the paranoid personality must be vigilant in order to safeguard himself against sudden deception and attack. He is exquisitely sensitive to traces of hostility, contempt, criticism or accusation. (p. 645)

From the standpoint of the paradox principle, paranoia is a constriction of trust. Whereas dependency and anxiety imply too little *self* trust, and phobia implies too little *environmental* trust, paranoia essentially implies too little *social* trust.

Let me close this section with a description of anorexia nervosa. Although a complex mingling of factors, anorexia is typified by a profound sense of guilt, shame, and the wish to remain small. The following case reported by Binswanger (1958b) is a dramatic illustration:

> "I didn't wish," Nadia said, "to become fat, or to grow tall, or to resemble a woman because I always wanted to remain a little girl." And why? "Because I was afraid of being loved less." (p. 333)

> [Nadia] flees from . . . others, would like to conceal herself from them, and suffers because she cannot do this as she would like. She is afraid to be conspicuous to . . . others, to be different from them, to be less loved by them, and she protects herself from all this by innumerable "devices". . . . These indications are only the breakthrough-points of an existence stricken by the curse of shame. (p. 337)

If paranoia is a constriction of trust, anorexia, in many cases, is a constriction of self-worth—especially as reflected in one's body. It is literally a bodily depression (see also Chernin, 1981).

Hyperconstriction can be summarized as the disproportional "carving up" of one's world. One either carves oneself into tiny pieces or surrenders to powers which perform the carving for one. In either case, one is centrically impoverished, atrophied, and choked off. One is barred from enrichment.

While this concludes the section on hyperconstriction, I want to point out that hypochondriasis, somaticization, avoidant personality, masochism, fetishism, and the abuse of substances which depress autonomic nervous system functioning—such as sedative-hypnotics—are also relevant to this polarity (see American Psychiatric Association, 1980; Becker, 1973; Khantzian, 1985; Kuhn, 1958).

HYPEREXPANSION

Mania, one of the most extravagant forms of expansion, is a "springing forth" as Binswanger (1975) put it, and a "leaping" from perspective to perspective. It is characterized by great bursts of movement, feeling, and intention. Binswanger (1975) elaborates:

> The disproportion evidenced in the manic pattern of life is spoken of daseinsanalytically as *flightiness*. It signifies the impossibility of obtaining a genuine foothold on the "ladder" of human problems, and in this respect, thus also signifies the impossibility of authentic decision, action, and maturation. . . . All too far and hastily driven *forward* and *carried upward* the manic hovers in fraudulent heights in which he cannot take a stand or make a "self-sufficient" decision. (pp. 346–347)

Mania, then, is the flipside of depression—the hyper*extension* of mood, perceived capability, and assertion.

Whereas mania expands and explodes one's *mood*, narcissism extends one's *self-image*. The essential feature of narcissism is "self-inflation" as Horney (1939, p. 89) put it. She goes on:

Psychic inflation, like economic inflation, means presenting greater values than really exist. It means that the
person loves and admires himself for values for which
there is no adequate foundation. Similarly, it means that
he expects love and admiration from others for qualities
that he does not possess, or does not possess to as large
an extent as he supposes. (pp. 89–90)

Among the other qualities identified as being narcissistic are "interpersonal exploitativeness," "expansive imagination," and "deficient social conscience"
(Millon, 1981, p. 166). The feature Binswanger termed
"greed" is also pertinent here:

The irrational trait of greed is precisely the Molochlike
quality which has, as a consequence, a definite spatial
interpretation of the world, that is, a strong emphasis
upon the significance of space which is filled up, se-
cluded, covered, and hidden; along with this, the body
is conceived as . . . hollow. . . . Time doesn't stand still
for the greedy. . . . Here time receives its meaning only
from images of snatching and filling. . . . Little spaces of
time are busily and constantly stuffed, as though in a
box. . . . What happens to time is that it becomes time
sums which can be added like bits and pieces. (quoted
in Sadler, 1969, p. 134)

Histrionic people display similar expansive qual-
ities.Their emphasis, however, is on social image, attention, and manipulativeness. Klein (1972) elaborates:

[Histrionics] are fickle, emotionally labile, irresponsible,
shallow, love-intoxicated, giddy, and short-sighted . . .
Seductive, manipulative, exploitative and sexually pro-
vocative, they think emotionally and illogically. Easy
prey to flattery and compliments . . . they are posses-
sive, grasping, demanding, romantic. . . . When frustrated or disappointed, they become reproachful, tear-

ful, abusive, and vindictive. . . . Rejection sensitivity is perhaps their outstanding common feature. (p. 237)

Shapiro (1965) adds that hysterical cognition is

impressionistic, relatively immediate, and global. The cognitive experience of the hysteric is an experience not of sharply observed facts and developed judgments, but of quick hunches and impressions. (p. 129)

Antisocial people are also quite dramatic, manipulative, and immediate. But they can be equally rebellious, violent, and reckless. Millon (1981) elaborates:

A major characteristic is what I would term "hostile affectivity"; this is illustrated by the fact that many of these personalities have an irascible temper that flares quickly into argument and attack. . . . Another characteristic . . . is . . . "social rebelliousness" as evidenced by the fact that these patients are contemptuous toward authority, tradition, sentimentality and humanistic concerns. . . . Another notable feature is their frequent fearless attitude in which many of them seem to be not merely undaunted by danger . . . but seem to provoke and be attracted to it. (pp. 182–183)

The body is an important feature of hostile affectivity. Stevick (1971) elaborates based on her study of anger.

The body is experienced as bursting forth, and expresses itself, publicly or privately as each person's pre-reflective restrictions allow, in expansive, explosive, non-typical behavior. (p. 144)

In addition to those syndromes described above, hyperexpansion appears to further encompass hyperactivity, attention-deficit, oppositionality, explosiveness, impulsiveness, and substance abuse associated with autonomic nervous system arousal, e.g., amphetamines and hallucinogens (see American Psychiatric Association, 1980; Binswanger, 1958a, 1958b; Khantzian, 1985; Kuhn, 1958; Prentky, 1979).

In summary, then, hyperexpansion is the ill-controlled propulsion, extension, or enlargement of one's experiential world. One either initiates these actions or perceives that the actions have been initiated by outside forces.

MIXED DYSFUNCTIONS
(CONSTRICTIVE/EXPANSIVE BLENDS)

Unlike the above unimodal gestalts, "mixed dysfunctions" are bimodal in character. Foucault (1965) captures the essence of these maladies:

> Tension and release, hardness and softness, rigidity and relaxation, congestion and dryness—these qualitative states characterize the soul as much as the body, and ultimately refer to a kind of indistinct and composite passional situation, one which imposes itself on the concatenation of ideas, on the course of feelings, on the state of fibers, on the circulation of fluids (p. 87).

Schizophrenia is perhaps the pinnacle of the mixed dysfunctions. Anyone who has dealt with schizophrenics has probably observed their enormous range of behavior. This shifts from pedantic and immobilizing obsessions to the most inflated psychophysiological states (Laing, 1969; Jaspers, 1963; Lowen, 1970; Sass, 1987, in press). Laing (1985) observes of one of his patients:

> He talked about . . . such things as prehistoric clairvoyance, problems of the infinitely small, interplanetary visitations floating as a sort of mist of consciousness in interstellar space. (pp. 141-142)

Binswanger (1958a) recapitulates:

> In many cases . . . it does not suffice to consider only
> *one* world design. . . . Whereas this serves our purpose
> in the morbid depressions, as in mania . . . in . . . what
> is known as schizophrenic processes we cannot neglect
> the bringing into focus . . . the various worlds in which
> our patients live. . . . In the case of Ellen West, for in-
> stance, we saw the existence in the shape of a jubilant
> bird soaring into the sky—a flight in a world of light and
> infinite space. . . . And, finally, we saw it in the form of
> a blind worm crawling in muddy earth, in the molder-
> ing grave, the narrow hole. (p. 209)[1]

Mark Vonnegut (1975), a "recovered" schizophrenic,
elaborates "first hand" on the syndrome:

> Small tasks became incredibly intricate and complex. It
> started with pruning fruit trees. One saw cut would take
> forever. I was completely absorbed in the sawdust float-
> ing gently to the ground, the feel of the saw in my hand,
> the incredible patterns in the bark, the muscles in my
> arm pulling back and then pushing forward. Everything
> stretched infinitely in all directions. Suddenly it seemed
> like everything was slowing down and I would never
> finish the limb. (p. 99)

Later, Vonnegut (1975) found himself "unable to stick
with any one tree. It seemed I had been working for
hours and hours but the sun hadn't moved at all" (p.
99). And in another passage he writes:

> Looking into the mirror I could see that my body had
> become a composite of all bodies. Half my face was
> Asian, an arm and a leg were black. But it was more

---

[1]Despite the controversy as to whether Ellen West was in fact schizophrenic (Arieti, 1974), Binswanger's general remarks about the syndrome, I believe, are phenomenologically sound.

subtle than that. Everything that had ever lived had
contributed their best cell to make what I now called me.
(pp. 150–151)

"Renee," finally, another highly articulate person af-
flicted with schizophrenia, had this to say:

> For me, madness was definitely not a condition of ill-
> ness. . . . It was rather a country opposed to Reality,
> where reigned an implacable light, blinding, leaving no
> place for shadow; an immense space without boundary,
> limitless, flat.

> People turn wierdly about, they make gestures, move-
> ments without sense; they are phantoms whirling on an
> infinite plain, crushed by the pitiless electric light. And
> I—I am lost in it, isolated, cold, stripped purposeless,
> under the light. (Sechehaye, 1970, p. 33)

"No one," concludes Laing (1967), "who has not
experienced how insubstantial the pageant of external
reality can be, how it may fade, can fully realize the
sublime and grotesque presences that can replace it, or
that can exist along side it" (p. 133).

What can be seen here is that a revolutionary insight into the structure of "psychopathology," indeed
Being, has been forged. For Laing, Vonnegut, Binswanger, and "Renee" expose empirically what earlier
philosophers, such as Kierkegaard, began to suspect:
schizophrenia can signify a battle of cosmological proportions. It can be a battle that transpires far beyond
any ordinary, or even extraordinary, boundary of life. It
can be a battle fought at the gateways to infinity—with
inconceivable minutiae and unremitting mass.

Schizophrenia, in such cases, is not so much a disease as a ripping open of the human condition, a portal
to every human potentiality—abysmal and grand. It
may be the final destination of the mind.

Was it not the "raving" Blake who wrote: "If the doors of perception were cleansed everything would appear as it is to man, infinite."

If *facing* chaos and minutiae is the plight of the schizophrenic, then skirting tremulously at the edges is the lot of the schizoid. Whereas the schizophrenic tangles with either *total* obliteration or *total* eruption, the schizoid appears to grapple with somewhat less conflict, or as Laing (1969) hinted, with separation vs. relation rather than "complete isolation or complete merging of identity (p.53)." "The schizoid," writes Guntrip (1969)

> becomes claustrophobic, and expresses this in such familiar ways as feeling restricted, tied, imprisoned, trapped, smothered, and must break away to be free and recover and safeguard his independence; so he retreats from object-relations. With people, he feels either bursting (if he is getting them into himself) or smothered (if he feels he is being absorbed and losing his personality in them). (p. 35)

While this scenario sounds strikingly like the "borderline" profile, there are two key distinctions: borderlines tend to be more social and emotional (Millon, 1981). Whereas the schizoid pervasively shrinks from social contact, the borderline periodically clamors for such contact; and whereas the schizoid tends to use cognitive defenses against bonding (suffocation) and separation (abandonment), the borderline tends to use emotional defenses (Guntrip, 1969; Millon, 1981). The borderline thus constricts into depression, self-hate, and dependency, and expands into hostility, manipulativeness, and impulsivity (Millon, 1981).

Degree of negativism appears to mark the difference between the above syndromes and the manic-depressive or bipolar experience (Binswanger, 1975). Whereas the schizoid and borderline appear hopeless about their fate, the bipolar individual clearly musters some optimism about his or her capabilities. Twisted as the manic-depressive may be, there is still the will to live (during the manic phase), the ability to force the psyche out of a "devitalized passivity" (Guntrip, 1969, p. 154; Kohut, 1977).

In addition to the above, there are a variety of other mixed dysfunctions—schizotypal, passive-aggressive, bulimic—which show similar ranges of withdrawal, depression, dependency, and overreactivity.

Chapter Three

THE BASIS FOR DYSFUNCTIONAL EXTREMES: BACKGROUND AND THEORETICAL ROOTS

The complex symbol of death is never [absent], no matter how much vitality and inner sustainment a person has.

—Ernest Becker

The polarity is between complete isolation or complete merging of identity rather than between separateness and relatedness. The individual oscillates perpetually between the two extremes, each equally unfeasible.

—R.D. Laing

Now that we have described the essential features of dysfunctional behavior, it is time to look at how it arises. How is it that people develop from pristine, delicate embryos into the troubled or even monstrous variety that emerges?

Despite the flood of research devoted to the "causes" of human suffering, such investigation continues to meet with quite limited success (Millon, 1981). One major reason for the inadequacy of our research is the complexity of the phenomenon. So many factors— both learned and genetic—appear to mediate its expression (Arieti, 1974).

However, another problem, which I believe is more resolvable, is that traditional psychology tends to study causal issues from a detached, preconceived framework

(Giorgi, 1970). For example, behavioral/cognitive research examines measurable behaviors only, and as a result, appears to miss important subjective factors (Merleau-Ponty, 1962; Giorgi, 1987). This explains the problem of reducing all behaviors to a stimulus and response, or to "self statements." "Johnny" may be afraid of snakes but it is quite likely that he is "put off" by a host of other factors as well (see Andrews, 1966; Green, Wilson, & Lovato, 1986; Wolfe, 1988). Depression, anxiety, and "health," moreover, mean a great deal more than percentages of positive and negative self-statements, as was suggested at a recent cognitive psychology seminar (Seligman, 1987). The human smile, finally, as Merleau-Ponty (1963) incisively demonstrated, is a vastly richer thing than positive reinforcement, or the contractions of the circumoral muscles. One has to wonder with Giorgi (1987) just how mainstream psychology could, to this day, fail to appreciate these issues.

It is not that behavioral concerns are inaccurate. Indeed, they have proven their usefulness (Smith, Glass, & Miller, 1980). The problem is that they are highly limited. They stop short of a fuller, more experiential understanding of consciousness. By the same token, psychoanalytic research, as we shall see momentarily, is restricted in certain profound respects, and fails to address the wider ranges of human expression (Arieti, 1976; Becker, 1973; Kohut, 1985, May, 1969).

In light of these problems, the following is an attempt to put forth hypotheses that can be tested phenomenologically, that is, with real people in real situations with as few preconceptions as possible. However, before we turn to the paradoxical basis for dysfunctional experience, let us develop the psychoanalytic backdrop from which it emerges.

PSYCHOANALYTIC LIMITATIONS

But there is another group of investigators of man's creative involve-
ment. . . . It consists mainly of academically based humanists who
for a variety of reasons have turned away from us in bitterness,
scorn, and ridicule. It seems they felt the insights we had to offer
them bypassed the essence of man . . . and dealt only with
peripheral trifles. It is to this latter group that the psychology of the
self now addresses itself.

—Heinz Kohut

It is to the great contributions of Freud and his successors that we owe so much in the field of developmental psychology. Freud (1961) adorned the psychical stage with three illuminating players: the id, the ego, and the superego. Without rehashing the details of these psychical functions, suffice it to say that they underpin many of our daily struggles. The id represents our surging instinctual drives (i.e., sex and aggression) which aim toward gratification; the superego refers to the moral standards that condition our instincts according to parental and social injunctions; and our ego is the mediator between the id and superego and tries to ensure that the expression of each is realistic and adaptive. Moreover, most of the personality, for Freud, is subconscious. Our egos permit us the only glimpses of awareness and control that we have. Maddi (1976) captured this doctrine well: "All . . . living has the aim of maximizing instinct gratification while minimizing punishment and guilt"(p. 34). Freudians might add, correlatively, that dysfunctional living is the result of an imbalance in this system, i.e., too little or too much instinct gratification.

Yet we must ask, with many other observers of the human scene, does the whole gamut of dysfunctional behavior really just come down to improper sexual and aggressive discharge? Is that what profound fear, hostility, anxiety, sadness, and elation are really all about? Is depression *fundamentally* the result of Oedipal guilt, the sense that our parents rejected us for longing for them sexually (see Freud, 1961)? Is this the essence of loneliness, self-loathing, helplessness, and immobility?

Or likewise, is mania *primarily* a counterreaction to this sexual guilt (see Freud, 1961)? Is this why I become socially and emotionally indulgent, speak, think, and move incessantly, and exaggerate my capabilities?

While such theories display a ring of truth, one is left discontent. For if depression, anxiety, mania, and the like are the mere products of improper sexual/aggressive discharge, then how does one explain their generalizing power, their depth and intensity (Klein, 1976)? Moreover, how does one explain the scanty support for *literal* interpretations of Freudian etiology (Fisher & Greenberg, 1985)? Dysfunctional behavior, it appears, is too intricate to be reduced to biological, sexual, or "stage-related" processes (Klein, 1976; Kohut, 1977; Millon, 1981; Stechler & Kaplan, 1980).

Rank (1936) (and later, object relation theorists, e.g., Guntrip, 1969; McDevitt & Mahler, 1980) extended the Freudian "drama" to earlier, and allegedly more basic psychical issues. This manifested itself in Rank's analysis of prenatal life and the life fear/death fear distinction.[1]

---

[1] I recognize that Rank's (1941) later work is underpinned by an even larger, more cosmic scope. That work, however, tends to lack cohesion, as Becker (1973) indicated, and leads in many ways to the direction I am formulating. My purpose here is to show how Rank's systematic thesis, which dominates neoanalytic thinking (see especially Guntrip, 1969), falls short of the present treatise.

Rank's (1936) basic thesis is that birth is the formative dilemma of an individual's life. The womb, for Rank, represents everything mysterious and unsettling. It is the dark abyss out of which life literally pours. Yet this abyss—as with postnatal life—is two-edged; unknown and untrodden, on the one hand, enclosed and secure on the other. The child is both terrified and enamored of these standpoints, and depending on the degree to which she is traumatized she is condemned to play one or the other out in subsequent activities. The drama revolves specifically around the "life and death fears" (Rank, 1936). The life fear is the dread of independence, of venturing out on one's own, of confronting the unfamiliar and transforming it in accordance with one's needs. The death fear is the revulsion for dependency, of uniting with the mother, of being swallowed up in her safeness and comfort, in her identity. Rank believed that both fears characterize our lives to one degree or another, and posed them as the wellsprings of dysfunctional action.

Jung (1966) produced an even broader synthesis.[2] His stress on the so-called collective unconscious has led to an even greater swell of interest and study. He believed that sex and aggression are only one aspect of a multifaceted conflict between historical myths (i.e., archetypes) on the one hand, and personal and social

[2]In order to clarify his emergence from Freud, I deal here only with Jung's "conflict" (as opposed to transpersonal) theorizing. I think this model comes closest (except perhaps for George Klein's psychoanalysis) to the existential view. However, it falls just short by overplaying mythic influences to the neglect of themes which underlie these influences, as I will show. As for the issue of transpersonal psychology, I will have more to say in the upcoming section on paradox and religion.

reality on the other. He designated masculinity (animus) and femininity (anima), old sages, starry-eyed adolescents, nurturing mothers, and tyrannical fathers as just a few of the diverse influences emanating from archetypal subconsciousness. Many of us deny these archetypes, Jung felt, because they threaten our ideals in some manner. They influence us to feel childlike while we are invested in adult responsibilities; or they make us feel maternal in spite of our conscious effort to appear sexy or businesslike, and so on. Yet, according to Jung, these "shadowy" or undeveloped potentialities cannot be totally denied. Unacknowledged and undealt with, the archetypes return in twisted and destructive forms, such as in the expressions of war and bigotry (Jung, 1966).

What we can see here is that both Rank and Jung are existentialists of sorts. They go beyond biologism. For example, Rank viewed the birth experience—the struggle for independence and assertion, along with dependency and mergence, as the templates for future functioning. Neuroses and psychoses, he believed, reflect a breakdown of this struggle. This breakdown occurs specifically in terms of either a fear of autonomy, which drives us into overdependency, as in the case of the depressed or passive-dependent person, or the fear of dependency, which prods us into profoundly estranged and hyperactive states, as in some forms of mania and schizophrenia.

Guntrip (1973) echoes Rank's view:

> The psychoanalytic researcher must go to the ultimate roots of the problem. . . . [G]rowth and ego consolidation begin, as Winnicott says, "at the beginning," with birth into the infant-mother relationship. Thereafter it proceeds through wider child-parent, scholar-teacher,

employee-employer, and marital relationships, and often needs to lead on into the patient-therapist relationship. (p. 150)

Correspondingly, Jung began with even earlier prenatal events. He envisioned, in accordance with several Eastern doctrines, that human beings are influenced by developments in their history, race, and culture. He contended that depression, anxiety, mania, and the like were the results of massive denial and overcompensation for these influences. For Jung, sadness, fear, and agitation translate into various combinations of mourning for, timidity toward, and frustration with one's mythic heritage.

Yet for all their revisionism, Rank and Jung failed to go far enough. They stopped unnecessarily short of an even fuller existential view. Thus, for example, underlying Rank's independence/dependence conflict appears to be the more basic dilemma between constriction and expansion. Fear of independence from the mother, for instance, can be seen as a fear of expanding *spatiotemporally*—exceeding the limitations of the body, the home, the terrain, the genes, the family, or culture. Moreover, that very same fear of independence can be viewed as a dread of retracting, of being segregated, isolated, and vanquished from space and time. Likewise, Rank's fear of dependence on the parent can be seen as a fear of surrendering, submitting, and subordinating oneself to the cosmic. It can also be seen as representing fears of unifying and ultimately merging with the cosmic (Schneider, 1986).

Jung's archetypes, similarly, can be broken down into constrictive/expansive aspects. The two important archetypes—anima (femininity) and animus (masculinity)—are illustrative. From the spatiotemporal perspective, anima can be seen as passive, quiet, fragile, soft, yielding, and reticent. It can also be viewed as engulfing, encompassing, swarming, smothering, merging, and fusing. The animus, correlatively, can be understood as restricted, focused, penetrating, isolating, and fragmenting. At the same time, it can be viewed as active, hard, bold, adventurous, and explosive (Jung, 1966; von Franz, 1975). Other Jungian archetypes such as the hero, the sage, the demon, the shadow, the earth mother, and the persona can be understood in similar spatiotemporal terms.

THE LIMITATIONS OF "SELF PSYCHOLOGY" AND "CLINICAL PSYCHOANALYSIS"

Recently, two overlapping psychoanalytic movements have attained prominence—"self psychology" and "clinical psychoanalysis." Self psychology arose out of the empathic-introspective observations of psychoanalysts and their patients (Kohut, 1977). Clinical psychoanalysis emerged from the direct observation of children and their caretakers (Klein, 1976; Stechler & Kaplan, 1980). Now although these movements—like those of Rank and Jung—criticize earlier analysts (e.g., for their biologism, historicism, and adultomorphism), existential psychology, I believe, awaits at the end of the road upon which they have just embarked.[3]

[3]Although the clinical psychoanalyst Klein (1976) criticizes the conscious, "here and now" emphasis of what appears to be Sartrian existential psychology (or "pop" versions thereof), he strongly acknowledges his debt—without actually making it explicit—to another strain of existential psychology. "The *dominant* thrust of existential thinking," he writes, "seems to me eminently consistent with psychoanalysis" (p.22). This thrust to which Klein refers, I

For instance, long before self psychology (see Klein, 1976; Kohut, 1977, 1985; Masek, 1986), existential psychology (1) overthrew Freud's physicalist-objectivist view of the person in favor of an empathic-introspective view (May, 1958; Binswanger, 1975); (2) addressed the contextual as opposed to reductionistic nature of consciousness (Merleau-Ponty, 1962); (3) showed the importance of future *intentions* for development in addition to that of past influences (Husserl, 1931; May, 1969); (4) pointed out the basic paradox of life—that we are free yet limited—and the resulting tensions, dynamics, and configurations that ensue from this condition (Becker, 1973; Kierkegaard, 1954; May, 1981; Heidegger, 1962); and most importantly, (5) developed a theory—which I am trying to make explicit—that anticipates the logical implications of self psychology. Let me explain.

The central drama of life, for self psychologists (as with clinical psychoanalysts), takes place between two poles: the subjective or autonomous and the objective or prohibitive (Kohut, 1977; Stechler & Kaplan, 1980). Autonomous strivings comprise temperaments, ambitions, and ideals, while prohibitions entail environmental (i.e., social, parental, physical) limits, rules, and standards. According to self psychologists, dysfunctional behavior results from an incompatibility between one's autonomous strivings and the prohibitions against them. A "firm," cohesive self, on the other hand, results from a consonance between such strivings and prohibitions (Kohut, 1977; Klein, 1976).

The problem with this "enlarged" psychoanalysis, however, is its failure to push through to the conclusion

---

believe, is existential-phenomenological psychology, and the basis for the paradox principle.

it anticipates. For, as we touched upon earlier, personal striving (taken to its peak) is more than just engagement of a need, talent, or value. It is more than a desire to be in control of one's *self*. It is, eventually, a desire to control or partake in the *cosmic design*, a striving for infinity or immortality (Becker, 1973; Kierkegaard, 1954; Yalom, 1980).

By the same token, the outside (or internalized) prohibitions against one's striving are more than just limits, rules, or standards. They are impositions (symbolically) of *infinite* demands, of a sense of having to confine, withdraw, assert, or incorporate *endlessly*.

The configuration of the self, then, does not end with the "self-object"—the individual and her parental, cultural, or even earthly surround (Kohut, 1977), but with the self-cosmic relation. What is at stake for the child is her ability to handle the *infinite* implications of every thought, feeling, and action, not just the social-familial implications. The *fundamental* psychodynamic issues are, does the child permit rejection to *obliterate* her? Does she face the *maximal* implications of her will? How adaptive are her defenses against (constrictive/expansive) *boundlessness?*[4]

Such issues embrace the very fabric of one's exis-

---

[4]When I speak of "boundless" here, I do not mean it in the Freudian or even neo-Freudian sense. These theorists define boundlessness as a regressed infantile state, in particular, a sexual or intra-uterine phenomenon (Sulloway, 1983; Guntrip, 1973). However, I see nothing inherently infantile about boundlessness. It is not the by-product of a certain period of development. It is the infinite background (extenuation) of *every* given experience. Although a child may be more vulnerable to its effects (i.e., due to weaker defenses), boundlessness must be seen as a *human* potentiality, ever-present and immediate (Becker, 1973; Merleau-Ponty, 1962).

tence. They are implicit not only in the way one approaches interpersonal relations but also in the way one approaches one's body, physical surroundings, vocation, cultural values, and so on (Merleau-Ponty, 1962). When I am sad, for example, I am sad bodily. Motion is threatening, and motor retardation is my only way to avert perceived exhaustion. I am sad visually. My world looks gray and drab. I am sad vocationally. Every paper I file, every thought I write down becomes an unfathomable burden and moves me closer to that expansive "otherness" that I fear. I am sad culturally. All my clothing, all my possessions, all my rituals appear painfully complicating and irrelevant.

Likewise, when I am angry I can hardly contain myself. My angry body defies anything that tries to restrain it. It lashes out at air, furniture, clothing. This is why I'm so susceptible to accidents when I'm mad. My angry eyes see in surrounding things agitation, sharp and jagged edges, obstacles to be subdued. Work, obligations, responsibilities of all sorts become "prison cells" from which I must break free. Minimization in any form becomes my enemy.

A related problem with self psychology is its lack of clarity about the dread and allure of human existence. Even Freud's model explained this better. Aside from Kohut's (1977) oxygen metaphors and allusions to omnipotence, self psychologists, and clinical psychoanalysts in particular, are never really explicit about the *terror* of blocked aims, or the appeal of fulfilled ones. Conversely, they are unemphatic about the appeal of prohibitions and the terror of self-fulfillment. In a phrase, self psychologists are never really explicit about the symbol of death for the human psyche. They do not take us to its farther reaches.

It should be clear from the foregoing, then, that "paradox" can provide a new basis for clinical observations, and that given this new framework, dysfunctional behavior serves a much broader, deeper cause. The basis for depression, hysteria, and the like is not ultimately instinctual nor even prenatal or interpersonal, but a more profound relation (Laing, 1969). We are sad or enraged, agitated or immobilized ultimately because our relationship with life, with the human condition, has been disrupted in some way. Our parents, birth canals, and myths symbolize wider networks. They are the bearers of cosmic messages—the media through which even more fundamental impressions are conveyed. They do not merely stifle or overstimulate our biological and sociocultural aims; they stifle or overstimulate the exercise of our potential—our longings to explore, manipulate, absorb, probe, and embrace the cosmos. They thwart or exaggerate our "affair" with life, and this includes many more concerns than copulation, assaultiveness, parental relations, and myth.

One of the strongest avenues of support for this revised view of psychoanalysis comes from clients themselves. The evidence is as apparent as daylight and yet conspicuously overlooked by most investigators. Perhaps this is so because the investigators themselves are as overpowered by the phenomenon as many clients appear to be (Yalom, 1980).

The phenomenon I refer to here is the catastrophic nature of clients' experiences. Clients convey that the worst part about their problem is that it appears endless and all-consuming, and that they, indeed the world, can do nothing about it. For example, "histrionics' need for recognition and approval appear *insatiable*" (Millon, 1981, p. 142, italics mine); antisocial personalities "behave as if softer 'emotions' [are] tinged with *poison*"

(Millon, 1981, p. 199, italics mine). Passive-aggressive persons "get into *endless* wrangles and disappointments as they vacillate between submissive obedience and conformity, at one time, and stubborn defiance and resolute autonomy, the next" (Millon, 1981, p. 217, italics mine). The shy person "*abhors* freedom with its lack of structure, its individual responsibility, and its many demands to act and initiate" (Zimbardo, 1977, p. 153, italics mine). The obsessional client's "disgust at decay, illness, germs, and dirt [is] intimately related to fear of personal *annihilation*" (Strauss quoted in Yalom, 1980, p. 49, italics mine).

Now the problem with these allegedly exaggerated perspectives is that, far from being *thought* "abberations," as cognitive psychologists are fond of contending (Beck, 1976; Ellis, 1962), they are startlingly accurate glimpses into *Being*. They are precise glimpses of the implications one faces the moment one acknowledges the horizonal nature of human experience (Merleau-Ponty, 1962)—the "gallery of mirrors" as Borges depicted (see Agheana, 1984). Every moment of anger, sadness, zeal, and fear implies the unbounded extension of those sentiments. The more I am aware of my anger, for example, the more I am aware of its connection to destructiveness and ultimately apocalypse. The more I am aware of my withdrawal, the more I am aware of vanishing. The more I am aware of my zeal, the more conscious I become of pandemonium. In short, the less *control* I have over my reflections, the more I unveil infinity.

Catastrophizing clients, then, are frightfully correct about the endlessness of cognitive, affective, and sensate experiences. This *is* the result of unbridled introspection and exteroception. The trouble is that one simply can't function with that degree of awareness.

The schizophrenic experience cogently supports the latter contention. Why is it, for example, that schizophrenics are often preoccupied by much more than biological and social concerns? Why is it that they recoil from invaders from other planets, or unseen particles and forces (Arieti, 1974)? Why is it that they are concerned with "beings which are far above us that [are] in charge and [are] running things" (Jesse Watkins quoted in Laing, 1967, p. 157), or with "stuff very much along the lines of what John Lilly . . . [wrote] about— consciousness, space, time, different levels of reality" (Laing, 1985, p. 139)? Finally, why is it, as one sufferer put it, that "balancing this illness is a matter of balancing opposites which are enormously incompatible" (Macdonald, 1979, p. 112)? Perhaps it is because schizophrenics are the ultimate catastrophizers, the least repressed individuals, and the most burdened psychically. Perhaps it is because they see—whereas most of us are unable to—that we are consigned not just to earthly but to as yet untold vistas and dimensions (Becker, 1973; Laing, 1967; May 1958a, 1958b; Sass, 1987).

After many years of clinical practice, Jaspers (1963) appears to concur:

> The "cosmic experience" is characteristic of schizophrenic experience. . . . "Everything" is always involved: all the peoples of the earth, all men, all the Gods, etc. The whole of human history is experienced at once. The patient lives through infinite millennia. The instant is an eternity to him. He sweeps through space with immense speed, to conduct mighty battles; he walks safely by the abyss. (pp. 294–295)

The experiences of those who take psychotomimetic drugs (drugs that mimic psychosis) add weight to the above literature (Bowers & Freedman, 1972). A person who takes mescaline, for example, appears to undergo a very distorted and magnified alteration of his "ordinary" consciousness. He is plunged, with this drug, into a world of "fluid" and oscillating forms, "intensified" interpersonal relationships, and sometimes overpowering "insights" (Bowers & Freedman, 1972, p. 482). He feels as if the "folds in [his] trousers" are "a labyrinth of endlessly significant complexity," or "the texture of the gray flannel," a "Botticelli picture" (Huxley, 1956, p. 30). Although he often considers such perceptions "inexpressibly wonderful," he also tends to be comforted by their transience and the benign setting in which he characteristically engages them (Bowers & Freedman, 1972; Huxley, 1956, p. 54). As he exceeds these bounds, however, as he approaches the unprotected schizophrenic intensities, that which was wonderful can readily shift into that which is "terrifying" (Huxley, 1956, p. 54).

To summarize, sex, aggression, parental relations, and archetypes all have constrictive and expansive contours which do not end. And it is this very endlessness, this ultimate condemnation to paradox, which both demolishes and, as we shall see later, propels the human spirit.

THE *PARADOXIC* UNDERSTANDING

The greatest fear in human beings is fear without end.
—J. Scott Rutan

So it is that we come to what I view as the basis for dysfunctional behavior—a resounding fear of the ulti-

mate expressions of infinity, space-time, or paradox
(see Becker, 1973). It is the result of our most ghastly
encounters with micropotential or macropotential, extension or confinement, and it is an experience or series
of experiences which prompt us to cave in, curl up, or
burst apart.

Let me be clear that I am speaking about more than
the dread of physical death here, but the dread of
"groundlessness," of being swallowed up (symbolically) in a "bottomless" pit, hole, or void (see
Yalom, 1980, p. 221; Sartre, 1957, p. 85). I am speaking
about a sense of *infinite* collapse, subordination, propulsion, or envelopment.

Thus, beyond father's or mother's punishing hand
(or the hand of the primal father, leader, or deity), beyond the stifling womb or mother archetype are the
infinity of associations relating to ultimate constriction.
For the victim, punishment and immobility conjure up
the entire range of constrictive images—isolation, entrapment, suffocation, diminishment, and ultimately
invisibility. They extend to one's deepest fears about
restraint, from the demeaning connotations of an oppressive hand or enclosure down to the murkiest feelings of being microscopic, unworthy, and invalid.

The range and impact of blocked expressions are
legion, and include, but are by no means limited to,
those of sexuality and aggression (Klein, 1976; Stechler
& Kaplan, 1980). There are family rules against chew-
ing, swallowing, eating, seeing, hearing, smelling, tast-
ing, touching, speaking, and even breathing in "disruptive" ways. Expansive feelings in many families (envy,
anger, contempt, joy, zeal, affection) are taboo. Likewise, expansive thoughts, such as early attempts to
question, abstract, philosophize, play, create, imagine,

and explore the world, are often squelched (Millon, 1981; Stechler & Halton, 1987).

While *parental* punishment and imposition of all sorts symbolize perhaps the most profound forms of constriction, there are many other environmental and personal events which can reflect this polarity. For example, how many of us have experienced the paralyzing fear of the neighborhood bully or gang leader? How many of us have had similarly domineering brothers, sisters, aunts, uncles, or grandparents? What about our oppressive experiences with teachers, doctors, administrators, and other social authorities (see Deleuze and Guattari, 1977)? What about our near madness regarding peer pressure and "impression management" techniques (see Goffman, 1959)?

Physical disorders too can exert numerous impositions on us. They can induce us to walk, talk, sense, eat, breathe, and move about in a myriad of confining and restrictive fashions. The lame must walk with extraordinary delay. The asthmatic must breathe with unusual care. The obese must sit and stand with apprehension. The visually impaired must be sure of their surroundings.

Indeed, the body in general can be a burdensome, subjugating machine (Lowen, 1970; Merleau-Ponty, 1962). Recall our early encounters with colds, flu, or fever—how restricted and victimized we felt. We couldn't play outside. We plodded tremulously about the house. We nauseously grabbed our stomachs and folded over. Remember, too, our reserve as we moved through the adult world. We ambled warily through super-sized rows of furniture and machinery. We stepped cautiously between colossal shoes and legs. We yielded to stifling commands and assertions. The helpless shock of one's early encounters with defecation, urination, ejaculation, or menses were further instances of perceived constraint. They proved as cumbersome as they could be freeing.

The mere fact of being limited physically and mentally could also be traumatizing to us—especially as children. We could only run so fast, fight so long, see so much. We could only throw, push, pull, lift, and grip so well. No matter how badly we desired otherwise, we could (and can) do only a *finite* amount.

Finally, catastrophic events such as earthquakes, floods, powerful storms, natural and mechanical accidents, military confrontations, and the like analogously impose great barriers on our behavior. This notion is brought home whenever we see the trapped and twisted victims of such upheavals, and the resources required to aid them.

By contrast, there are many events, including aspects of those above, which engender fears of ultimate expansion, recklessness, tumult, and ultimately chaos. We are alarmed, for example, by our parents' physical powers. We see them lifting massive objects. We feel them twirl us in midair. We blink as their muscles bulge or arms flail. We stagger before their bold, pungent odors, and their radiant sensuality. We cower before their mental vigors—their grand pronouncements and plans, their staggering emotional outbursts, their awesome convictions and responsibilities.

We shiver before the extensive obligations and demands they place on us—the pressure to appear before crowds, entertain family or friends, laugh and fight as they laugh and fight, look pretty, "dress up," be "happy," be proud, make money, buy things, get a job, get a spouse, get a house, and become everything that *they* want us to become (Miller, 1981).

We panic at our own physical and mental churnings—our first ghostly nightmares; our terrifying encounters with darkness or being lost; our wrenching expulsions of blood or vomit; our shock at scary movies, stories, people, and places.

Other environmental events, such as powerful machinery—rockets, tanks, jets, bombs, automobiles—can also reflect the above associations. How many times have we recoiled at the sensation of speed, thrust, and acceleration? What about the terrifying dazzle of grand buildings, monuments, and shrines—the earth too with its jagged and active terrains, swelling oceans, and jolting climatic changes. The full assortment of upheavals, disasters, and accidents can also engender our fears of the expansive. For example, how many times have we cringed before car crashes, or quivered during large demonstrations or gatherings.

Thus, given the constrictive or expansive bases for our fears, how is it that they blow up into clinical syndromes? How is it that they lead to dysfunctional living? We can now turn to such an examination.

DEVELOPMENTAL PARADOXES

As has been shown, the child is born into a divided yet wide-ranging world. He or she is both limited and free, and has the capacity to tap either mode to a realistic degree. Yet reality and realistic possibility is the province of the functional. The dysfunctional's world, by contrast, has been mercilessly marred. His or her capacity to act and feel has become estranged and one-sided. We have already described what this one-sidedness looks like in people, for example, hyper-constrictiveness, hyperexpansiveness, or dysfunctional mixtures of the two. We have also noted some spatiotemporal themes which appear to give impetus to such personality outcomes, for example, as fear of diminishment and fear of cataclysm. Now we must put the picture together. We must ask, in what specific ways does the fear of infinity promote human destructiveness?

To begin with, the child is confronted by two basic influences at birth: temperament, sometimes called disposition, and environment, often characterized by parental interactions (Thomas & Chess, 1977). These early influences are critical with respect to the child's subsequent internalizations and self-concept (Erikson, 1963; Thomas & Chess, 1985). From the standpoint of the paradox principle, the child's temperament and surroundings can be distilled into constrictive and expansive themes. The child may express (though sometimes awkwardly) any of a range of constrictive or expansive movements, vocalizations, fantasies, needs, sensations, or urges (see Erikson, 1963, pp. 403–420).

Now it is of crucial importance in those earliest years (1) how the child perceives himself or herself (i.e., his or her temperament); (2) how the child perceives the surroundings, especially caretakers; and (3) the extent to which those perspectives are compatible (Erikson, 1963; Klein, 1976; Stechler & Kaplan, 1980; Thomas, Chess, & Birch, 1968).

Let us look at some simple case illustrations of this perceptual matrix. The following represent a range of contrasts between childhood expectations and perceived environmental offerings regarding need for affiliation. A child could feel a (relatively) low need and perceive the surroundings as *acutely* overgratifying. A child could feel a low need and experience the surroundings as *relentlessly* over-gratifying. A child could feel a high need and perceive the surroundings as *acutely* rejecting. The child could feel a high need and perceive the surroundings as *relentlessly* rejecting. Finally, a child could feel a high or low need and perceive the surroundings as *justly* gratifying.

The preceding combination bears careful examination, for it is just such a scenario that supports the entire dysfunctional (and functional) edifice. What we see here is that a child can view his or her inclinations and milieu in any of a range of comparative magnitudes. We shall now see that it is those very contrasts between felt disposition and milieu, necessity and possibility, that combine to produce the dysfunctional profile. Let me now propose five basic outcomes which arise out of the perceptual matrix: acute, chronic, and implicit trauma, denial, and overcompensation.

Acute trauma is the perception of an event as *immediately* contrary and shocking (see Erikson, 1963, on "counterphobia" and Stechler & Halton, 1987, on "oppositions"). It is an existential jolt which produces extreme fear. For example, when a child perceives her need for affiliation as sharply opposed, the child becomes extremely fearful that her need will not be expressed. If the trauma is impressive enough, it tends to lead to denial, which is the next phase in the dysfunctional sequence. *Denial* is defined as the refusal to accept or become aware of the events one fears (see Stechler & Halton, 1987). In this case the child would deny that her need for affiliation is being opposed, and would likely increase or overcompensate for this very fact. *Overcompensation* is defined as the fearful, escapist counteraction of trauma. Acute trauma produces acute (i.e., directly counteractive, oppositional) overcompensation. The child in the latter case, for example, would probably overcompensate for her trauma by increasing her cries for contact (Erikson, 1963; Stechler & Halton, 1987).

Let us look at this sequence in terms of constriction and expansion. The child perceives parental rejection (e.g., a strict command) as an oppressive (constrictive) force. This force has the effect of overpowering and crushing the child's urge for affiliation (expansive reaching out). Her desire being squelched, the child then collapses in a terrifying psychophysiological withdrawal (constriction). This entrapped, confined state is so repugnant to the child that it conjures up fears not just of being rejected but of morbid diminishment as well. In order to survive, the child must massively deny these experiential implications. She must begin the process not only of selectively inattending, as Sullivan (1953) framed it, but also of fervent opposition (Adler, 1927; Stechler & Halton, 1987). Accordingly, the child moves to what she perceives as the least threatening perceptual position. Given the acuteness of the child's trauma in our example, this position takes the form of searing cries and demands. To summarize, an expansive field (i.e., a parental command) constrained a less expansive field (i.e., a child's neediness). The less expansive field then retracted in response. This state, however, was so discrepant with the familiar (centric) position that the child, in turn, warped into hyperexpansion to overcompensate. Stechler & Halton (1987) report a similar sequence with regard to a child's assertive tendencies:

> Hannah has not received much support for her assertion and self-development during her first two years. She is an active baby, and mother exhibits little understanding of her feelings and states. . . . Mother often feels overwhelmed . . . as she ineffectually tries to control or prohibit Hannah's plans by shouting or hitting. . . . Before the age of one year, Hannah attacks mother by biting and punching her, and in the second year, they frequently hit each other. (p. 832)

Acute trauma can also bring about hyperconstrictive consequences. For example, a child who may view herself as relatively shy and retiring encounters circumstances in which she is required to assert herself or lead others. If this requirement is discrepant enough with her original disposition, she will probably counterreact and become even more shy and withdrawn (Stechler & Halton, 1987; Zimbardo, 1977, pp. 61–62).

It should be evident by now that acute trauma can have many antecedents and effects. Children can feel traumatized by perceived anger, fear, sadness, anxiety, and even joy. Moreover, they can feel traumatized by other environmental or personal events (e.g., disease, poor housing, crime, poverty, abundance, or spiteful neighbors). The issue hinges on the degree to which surrounding events differ from children's expectations of those events (Thomas & Chess, 1985). As a general principle, the more that surrounding events are felt to oppose one's impulses, the more they are perceived as deathlike and traumatic. The more that events are viewed as traumatic, the more one is likely to take the path of least resistance and counterreact (see Kohut, 1977; Shapiro, 1965).[5]

Chronic trauma is the sense of *unabating* opposition by environmental forces, the sense that one cannot effectively counteract or escape from environmental pressures. Whereas acute trauma often results in immediate counteraction, chronic trauma tends to produce a long-term inability to counteract. For example, persistent rejection of a needy child's quest for affection will eventually decrease rather than increase the child's ability (and desire) to oppose and overcompensate for the rebuffs (see Miller, Rosellini, & Seligman, 1977, on "learned helplessness," Bettelheim, 1960, on concentration camp victims, and Vaillant, 1977, on continuously disturbed relationships).

It is at this point that a curious shift occurs. Having been relentlessly denied, the child will ironically begin to view the original aim (i.e., affection) to be less desirable than the blockage of that aim (i.e., forced quiescence). Thus our child will have become so repulsed by the aberrant consequences of her original plea for affection that she will in turn acquiesce to the parental demand. I call this forced internalization of an environmental press a *traumatic shift*. The trauma is shifted from

[5]Although most counteractions of acute trauma are swift and immediate, this is not always the case. Sometimes victims are able to effectively suppress their initial traumatic encounters, only to preoccupy themselves with them weeks or even years later (see Lifton, 1976 on "psychic numbing"). Such experiences of delayed acknowledgment are characteristically termed, "posttraumatic stress symptoms" (American Psychiatric Association, 1980). These symptoms include flashbacks, nightmares, intensive guilt feelings, and rage reactions, and appear to represent (albeit in belated form) the underlying constrictive or expansive perceptions.

the once repulsive blockage of the aim to the aim itself. Whereas the thwarting (constriction) of the aim for affection was the basis for acute trauma, the expression (expansion) of the aim becomes the basis for chronic trauma. Thus the child eventually learns to overcompensate for the morbidity associated with the original expansive aim, by increasing her ability to constrict or inhibit that aim. It is possible that chronically traumatized children will end up more fervently opposed to their original aims than were their parents (see Spitz, 1965, on the identification with the aggressor phenomenon).

We see many examples of chronic trauma in everyday life. There are numerous people who have been so rebuffed, so beaten down in their attempts to express themselves that those attempts atrophy. They begin to associate their desire for a fuller life with more trepidation than the suspension of that desire. Some of the most depressed, despondent, and compliant lives result from such "learned helplessness" (Bettelheim, 1960; Miller, Rosellini, & Seligman, 1977; Stechler & Halton, 1987; Vaillant, 1977). The following childhood case is illustrative:

> Ned has an extremely prohibiting family system, starting in the first year. Ned is playing with a rattle, and when he puts it in his mouth, mother quickly removes it. When he goes to the side of the crib and holds on to the bars, mother takes his hands away from the bars and moves him back to the center of the crib. . . . As Ned crawls around the kitchen at ten months, mother uses shame to control his behavior. "Now what have you done?"

> At about sixteen months, following an intermittent series of infectious illnesses, Ned starts to lose his initia-

tive and becomes inhibited and fearful. From this point on, any resistance offered by Ned is essentially passive. (Stechler & Halton, 1987, pp. 833–834)

The investigators' comment:

Unlike many other children who are faced with partial prohibitions, and who are able to find some area of acceptable active pursuits, Ned was ultimately thwarted because it was not specific assertions such as exploring the house, or controlling the feeding that were objected to by his mother. Rather, it was the *idea* of his assertiveness *per se* that she could not abide. (Stechler & Halton, 1987, pp. 835–836)

People can also be chronically traumatized in the expansive direction. This could result, for example, if one initially feels reserved but confronts what are perceived as incessant demands to affiliate. After many years of this kind of subjugation, the child internalizes the parental demands and comes to see his former needs as reproachful. He begins to disdain constriction (isolation) and seeks expansive alternatives. Again, such people are visible in daily life, for example, cult members and children of families that forced them to be beauty queens or movie stars (see Miller, 1981; Spitz, 1965).

There is one last point to be made about the victims of chronic trauma. Although most such children fully internalize that which is demanded of them, a few do not. Some children, for example, while outwardly conforming to what is required, inwardly rebel. These children and later, adults, are characteristically termed "dissociative." They find every psychological means necessary, including the creation of multiple personalities, to escape their dreaded compliance (Millon,

1981). The problem with such people, however, is that their strategies, too, often result in extremism, and require a great deal of "redress" to undo.

Let us turn now to the issue of implicit trauma, which is a much subtler and probably more pervasive dysfunctional precursor than either of the above two. *Implicit trauma* is the indirect, vicariously learned revulsion for an experience or event (see McGoldrick & Gerson, 1985; Millon, 1981; Bandura, 1977). Implicit trauma, as opposed to acute or chronic trauma, is never directly confronted by the individual; rather it is transmitted to the individual through others—usually generations of others such as parents and grandparents—who are highly influential to the individual. The reasons for this influence are no doubt variable, and in need of further exploration. However, one explanation is apparent: If the offspring's temperament is similar to that of the perpetrator(s), he will more likely model, rather than resist, the received patterns of behavior (Bandura, 1977). Imitation, then, is the chief mode through which children become implicitly traumatized, and temperament is one determinant of the child's willingness to imitate (see Asher, 1987).[6]

In the case of our needy child, for example, the following illustrates implicit trauma: The child senses herself as expansive (i.e., deeply affiliative) and she is born into a correspondingly hyperexpansive house-

___

[6]The idea that psychological dispositions can be transmitted psychologically, as well as genetically, adds weight to the role of the environment in development. While it may be true that in many instances drinking and depression are genetically marked, the *fears that predate* such dispositions may well insure their actualization (McGoldrick & Gerson, 1985).

hold. Both parents are flamboyant, impulsive, and indulgent. Further, we see that this polarization did not begin merely with the present generation. With the aid of a genogram we find that it dates back several generations. My hunch is that if we could trace this polarization back far enough, with enough detail, we could specify its traumatic core (see McGoldrick & Gerson, 1985). For example, we might find that a painful sense of hyperconstriction disposed an influential ancestor to hyperexpand. This could mean, therefore, that the ancestor was acutely traumatized. He was originally disposed toward expansion, confronted a highly constrictive force (i.e., a harsh parent or disease), and overcompensated by fleeing into even greater expansion than he had been disposed to originally. The ancestor's influence, in turn, spread out to succeeding generations.

Of course, the "core" trauma could also have been acutely expansive (as in the case of a shy ancestor who confronts an overwhelming demand to socialize). In this case, succeeding generations would probably dwell under the shadow of deeply constrictive tendencies such as excessive aloofness, conservatism, and secretiveness. On the other hand, chronic trauma may underlie the familial disposition. For example, an impressionable ancestor could have been so browbeaten by an opposing force that he finally allied with it, and completely redirected the original fear. Each of the above (as well as unexplained genetic dispositions) could produce the basis for implicit trauma, and the highly dysfunctional lifestyles which result.

As can be seen, these scenarios are complex and varied. The key point here is that dysfunctional behavior stems from the dread of the "death," nonbeing,

Purported Operation of Three Traumatic Cycles

Type of trauma	Subject's disposition	Perceived environmental demand	Purported psychological effect on subject
Acute	Constrictive	Expansive	↑ Constriction
	Expansive	Constrictive	↑ Expansion
	Neutral*	Expansive	↑ Constriction
	Neutral	Constrictive	↑ Expansion
Chronic	Constrictive	Expansive	↑ Expansion
	Expansive	Constrictive	↑ Constriction
	Neutral	Expansive	↑ Expansion
	Neutral	Constrictive	↑ Constriction
Implicit	Constrictive	Constrictive	↑ /= Constriction
	Expansive	Expansive	↑ /= Expansion

Note. ↑ means increased constriction or expansion relative to one's disposition. ↑ /= means about the same or an increased degree of constriction or expansion relative to one's disposition. *"Neutral" means relatively nonpolarized.

or endlessness one perceives to oppose one. Either "death" becomes associated with extreme constriction or expansion, and one will do anything one can—including becoming extreme oneself—to flee such polarities (see Becker, 1973, 1975; Lifton, 1969, 1976; Yalom, 1980, for comprehensive reviews on the empirical evidence for the fear of death). (See the table on page 85 for a summary of the forms of trauma, their purported bases, and effects.)

CASE SUMMARIES OF THE FORMS OF TRAUMA

I will now illustrate the acute, chronic, and implicit traumatic matrices with my own and others' case material. These summaries are intended to be suggestive—rather than exhaustive—with respect to the roots of real-life suffering.*

Case I: Acute Trauma

A 12-year-old female client whom I'll call Kate glided confidently into my office. Her clothes and bearing were understated—not atypical for this rural, midwestern town.

Kate was the oldest of five children and apparently the most troublesome. Her presenting problems were formidable—hostility, oppositionality, resistiveness,

---

*A word to my former clients: I am deeply appreciative for what we have shared, and for the help your experiences can provide others. To ensure the confidentiality of our work, I have carefully disguised your names and circumstances. Those readers who think they can identify particular clients are probably mistaken.

minor scraps with the law, destructiveness (toward property, others, and self), and truancy. Kate was a truly unsettling individual. Her quiet unassuming manner belied an imminent sense of explosiveness. From birth, Kate's temperament appeared to have been irritable and demanding. As she "matured," her family circumstances worsened. At six, her alcoholic mother deserted the family, and by eight, her father, who was a disabled veteran, had remarried. However, the woman he married had allegedly abused a daughter from a previous marriage and appears to have been sadistic toward Kate and her siblings. For example, Kate's father reported that the stepmother would play a game with the children in which they were tied together by their ankles. She would also punish them, reportedly, by directing them to lie face down on the floor for an hour. If they moved, according to Kate's father, she would force them to do the same thing except this time with a 25-pound weight on their backs. Although the father soon divorced the stepmother, it was clear that neither he nor the children would forget her.

Kate's father also exhibited problematic behavior toward Kate. In addition to receiving psychiatric help for "moodiness" and overreactivity to stress, he appeared very ambivalent toward her. On the one hand, he showed great interest in her welfare, sometimes to the point of pampering her. On the other hand, he appeared contemptuous of her. This latter sentiment is illustrated by his tolerance (tacitly, as it may have been) of his wife's abusive behavior and of his intolerance of Kate's resemblance to her mother, whom he disdained.

Kate's sense of *global* rejection and the measures she took to counteract that perception became increasingly evident during my work with her. She sat at a conspicuous distance from me, often challenging me or attempting to provoke me with her stares. She denied any and all culpability for her problems. She described what most people would consider to be shocking actions (playing with guns, fire, razors, needles, knives) in a completely indifferent fashion. She left home and "did what she wanted" for days.

I have many more memory flashes of Kate: her consummate fascination with speed and explosives; her worship of criminals and the practitioners of martial arts; her contempt for teachers and rules; her yen for retribution and revenge; and her zeal for mayhem and mischief—actions which flaunt convention.

What this profile suggests is that Kate was a victim of acute trauma. She began with a relatively irritable (expansive) temperament that was then quashed several times by autocratic and apparently sadistic parenting. However, this parenting style appears not to have been of sufficient frequency, duration, and intensity to eradicate Kate's tendencies (recall her father's inconsistencies and her stepmother's brief contact). Kate resisted it, therefore, and hardened to its effects. Her fear of being squelched, of being minimized and eviscerated, was given periodic "holidays," which afforded her time to replenish her defenses. What inadvertently became nurtured over time was a veritable one-girl battle station, complete with wartime regalia. Kate became an unguided human missile and each step of her evolution an unwitting partisan to that peculiarity.

I made only partial headway with Kate. She was too far gone by the time I saw her, and ended up in residential treatment. But her expansiveness, I must say, has always intrigued me and given me glimpses, I believe, into apocalyptic realms.

Case II: Chronic Trauma

I met Gloria at a very grievous period of her life. She was 26, episodically alcoholic, and chronically distressed. She lived with her father and brother (her mother had left when she was a child) in a dilapidated, impoverished section of town.

According to reports, Gloria had been a very lively baby and young child. She had an appetite for sports, made friends readily, and received much attention for her "tomboyish" good looks, scholarship, and athletic prowess.

However, at about nine years of age, Gloria's world shattered. She underwent a liver operation which required that she return to the hospital several times for one- to two-month stays. By age eleven, Gloria had fractured her skull in a freak ice-skating accident, which necessitated that a large metal plate be inserted in her head, and even more hospitalizations. Subsequently, Gloria became epileptic and required regular doses of antiseizure medication.

Meanwhile, Gloria's father began to dote on her excessively. He brought her food and clothing and sat with her for hours, often days, in her hospital room. Gloria's father allegedly began to look upon her as a helpless infant whom only he could rejuvenate. At the same time, he himself became increasingly depressed and began requiring psychiatric treatment and hospitalization.

As Gloria moved into adolescence, she too became increasingly depressed. She no longer readily spoke or met with friends. She could no longer play sports or obtain good grades. She became increasingly withdrawn and began to stammer when she spoke. She became self-loathing and greatly worried about her abilities. She also became increasingly dependent upon her father, yet began to resent him for not allowing her to grow up. She felt like a "daddy's girl" and thought that her neighbors—who were very "street tough"—were making fun of her. She developed a great deal of suspicion and hostility toward these neighbors, and yet could not find the heart or energy to express it.

By the time I saw Gloria, she was a depressed, anxious, alcohol-dependent, sexually inhibited, suspicious woman. She spoke very haltingly, and was almost desperate to form words. She said she had undergone a series of unhelpful psychiatric treatments. She reported being greatly misunderstood, confused, and scared, and that she had contemplated suicide (which she had attempted several years before) as a way out.

What is apparent here is that Gloria is the victim of a relentless chronic trauma. Her early exuberance, tragically, only served to set up false expectations. Her joy, her activities, her accomplishments boasted proudly only to be smashed by contravening events. The liver operation, the skull fracture, the hospitalizations, and even her father's love came rambling over her like a truck flattening a flower bed. Gloria was leveled, and although she resisted at first and fought like hell to pump the life back into herself, she could not do it. She was effectively "crushed" too many times.

By the time Gloria and I ended therapy, we were witness to some very hopeful changes. She had ceased to drink, her speech was more clear and affable, she acquired a full-time job, and she formed plans to move into her own apartment. The sad twist, however, was that just before our final day together, Gloria severely injured a woman while riding her bicycle. Apparently it was an accident, but Gloria took it very hard and made a suicidal gesture when the police contacted her for questioning. She was subsequently placed back in psychiatric treatment, only to desert it soon thereafter. Although she continued to resist treatment, she is reportedly "managing" in the community.

I have often wondered, since that time, about the weight of the burdens that Gloria now carries in her life. No matter how many times she attempted to "stand," it seemed something or someone would knock her back down. Either fate, her father, or her own body would appear to fail her at critical periods. How many of us have known similar circumstances? How many of us could testify as well to the awesomeness of existential forces and the ardor required to combat those forces?

Implicit Trauma: Case Overviews

The following is a summary, both anecdotal and empirical, of "breaks" (or "myths" as Zilbach, 1979, p. 77 calls them) in the family operation that harden and impose their mark across many generational lines (see Bowen, 1978; McGoldrick & Gerson, 1985; Laing, 1971; Zilbach, 1979). Families, for example, can perpetuate myths of expansive invulnerability, dominance, vengefulness, sociability, and achievement. They can also promote myths of constrictive submissiveness, isolation, timidity, conservatism, and rigidity. They can further display wide variations and combinations of these and other characteristics (Zilbach, 1979). Let us look now at several dysfunctions that have appeared to have arisen in such contexts.

The Adams family (who spawned two presidents)

fostered a standard of great and, in many cases, unattainable success. This standard pervaded four generations and may have been responsible for incompetence and suicide in those who could not meet it (McGoldrick & Gerson, 1985).

Playwright Eugene O'Neill's ancestry was also characterized by depression and suicide. O'Neill's mother was a morphine addict, his brother drank himself to death, and his eldest son committed suicide (McGoldrick & Gerson, 1985).

With regard to intergenerational "anniversary reactions," Henry Fonda's son Peter shot himself in the stomach less than a year after his mother committed suicide; and actress Margaret Sullivan's daughter committed suicide a year after her mother did (McGoldrick & Gerson, 1985).

Intergenerational child abuse has also received a considerable amount of attention. This research suggests that child abusers themselves are the victims of abuse, and that such practices can cross many generational lines (Achenbach, 1982; Patterson, 1986).

Finally, there is some indication that schizophrenia, in certain circumstances, can be psychologically transmissible. McGoldrick & Gerson (1985, p. 113) discuss an instance of schizophrenia which may be partly due to extreme intergenerational "imbalance" (e.g., "fused" son-mother dyads, "distant" son-father dyads, and "distant" or conflictual father-mother dyads). This pattern appears to have persisted through several generations and to have confused, bewildered, and maddened several generations of males. Laing (1971) discusses similar (albeit even more perplexing) cases from his investigations.

Now it is helpful to ask, why are some children more susceptible to implicit trauma than others? While there is, as yet, no clear answer to this question, the research does point to interesting alternatives. In particular, it appears that temperamentally *agreeable* children, or those most similar to their parents, are the likeliest to imitate them. One implication of the McGoldrick and Gerson work is that productive or successful children broke away from their family influences (at least for substantial periods),whereas less successful children emphatically succumbed to these influences (see also Bandura, 1977, on childhood modeling behaviors).

In summary, substantial numbers of dysfunctional people have been implicitly traumatized. Fear is familial, generational, and radial in addition to being very personal. Some of those implicitly traumatized don't even recognize their problem until it is too late. The paradox principle, it is hoped, can help others to avoid this fate.

Taken together, acute, chronic, and implicit traumas can unveil a wide range of dysfunctional dynamics. Dysfunctional constriction, for example, can now be understood in terms of the expansive forces that are perceived to oppose it. For example, because they had caved in on her, Gloria became terrified of her assertiveness, emerging womanhood, and independence. She developed depression, dependency, and suspiciousness as a result. People who dread flexibility, ambiguity, and diversity, similarly, may become obsessional (see Becker, 1973; Millon, 1981; Shapiro, 1965); some who fear interpersonal commitment (at a basic level) may become paranoid (Shapiro, 1965); some who link trauma with self-assurance may become anxious (see May, 1977); some who are repulsed by ambition and sensuality may become anorexic (Binswanger, 1958b; Chernin, 1981); and so on.

Hyperexpansion, likewise, can be explained by this

model. Kate's horrifying encounters with vulnerability, intimacy, and rules drove her into hostility and recklessness. Some manic clients, similarly, appear to dread restrictiveness and despondency (see Guntrip, 1969; Kohut, 1985); histrionics, detail and routine (see Millon, 1981; Shapiro, 1965); impulsives, deliberation and delay (Shapiro, 1965); and narcissists, humility and vulnerability (Millon, 1981; Kohut, 1977).

Indeed, many of our "everyday" problems can be explained by this model. The fear of *confinement*, for example, has probably led many of us to become gluttons, to rebel unnecessarily, and to demean or spite others. The fear of *extension*, conversely, has probably led many of us to become rigid, narrow-minded, petty, passive, or retiring.

The implication here is that we are now in a position—perhaps better than ever before—to understand the relevant bases of peoples' concerns. We no longer have to limit ourselves to "drives" and social prohibitions but can survey the myriad aims, compulsions, and dispositions that oppose given dysfunctions (as well as moment to moment polarizations) (see Klein, 1976; Stechler & Kaplan, 1980). In short, we can move more rapidly to the *sources* of people's fears, and work with them in their immediate, *lived* contexts.

Mixed Dysfunctions

Let us turn now to the development of dysfunctionally mixed or bipolar people. Although the evidence is less firm here, there is some indication that such people suffer from some kind of alternating traumatic pattern. This pattern appears to entail profound inconsistencies and double-binds. For example, "mixed" persons may evolve in such a manner that they feel jolted by constriction at one point and jarred by expansion at another. If this happens intensively enough over a long enough period of time, a constrictive/expansive swing may be set into motion.

Passive-aggressive personality styles, for instance, appear to arise from inconsistent parenting patterns. Millon (1981) states that the parents of passive-aggressives

> may have been in deep and continuing conflict regarding their attitude toward and their handling of these children. The parents may have been quite different from each other in their personality styles, thereby providing highly divergent and contradictory models for vicarious learning. They may have been inconsistent themselves, having swayed from hostility and rejection, at one time, to affection and love at another. (p. 266)

Borderline patients, similarly, appear to have been even more conflicted about separation/relation issues. Millon (1981) elaborates on what he terms the "borderline-passive-aggressive" profile:

> The negativistic, discontented, and erratic quality of these patients is largely attributable to early parental inconsistency. Most failed to be treated in even a moderately predictable fashion, being doted upon one moment and castigated the next—ignored, abused, nurtured, exploited, promised, denied, and so on, with little rhyme or reason as they saw it. (p. 366)

Schizophrenics, finally, appear to have undergone the most contradictory developmental experiences (see Zilbach, 1979, for a review). This appears to be true even for some with strong genetic dispositions (Arietti, 1981). Laing (1971) observes of his schizophrenic clients: "They are deeply immobilized in a complex knot, both internal and external, of contradictory, paradoxical attributions and injunctions" (p. 52).

The double-bind communication as Bateson *et al.* (1956) and later Laing (1961, 1967) elaborated on it, is a case in point. In double-bind communication a loved one (usually the parent) conveys to the child

> that he should do something, and at the same time conveys on another level that he should not, or that he should do something else incompatible with it. The situation is sealed off for the 'victim' by a further injunction forbidding him or her to get out of the situation, or to dissolve it by commenting on it. The 'victim' is thus in an 'untenable' position. He cannot make a move without catastrophe. (Laing, 1961,p. 146)

Laing (1961, p. 146) goes on to give a vivid illustration of this situation drawn from the Bateson *et al.* (1956) study:

> A mother visits her son, who has just been recovering from a mental breakdown. As he goes toward her
> a) she opens her arms for him to embrace her, and/or
> b) to embrace him
> c) As he gets nearer she freezes and stiffens
> d) He stops irresolutely
> e) She says, 'Don't you want to kiss your mummy?'— and as he still stands irresolutely
> f) she says, 'But dear, you mustn't be afraid of your feelings.'

Such examples illustrate that some children—due either to their own hypersensitivity, family peculiarities, or both—become horribly confused by what is expected of them. The confusion impresses upon the child that to approach (e.g., extend, embrace, trust) is to flirt with his own dissolution or loss of independence. It can also imply that he will intractably fuse with the other and, ultimately, Being (Laing, 1969).

The third implication is that to avoid, separate, and distrust is to invite equal dissolution (e.g., deprivation, isolation, fragmentation) or, on the expansive end, pandemonium (e.g., turbulence, recklessness, and ultimately chaos) (Laing, 1969).

It is perhaps no wonder, then, why such children learn to clang words together, leap from subject to subject, meld into people or things, and shudder at life. They are literally terrified to take a stand. Laing (1969) concludes that such children

> come to live like those mechanical toys which have a positive tropism that impels them towards a stimulus until they reach a specific point, whereupon a built-in negative tropism directs them away until the positive tropism takes over again, this oscillation being repeated *ad infinitum*. (p. 53)

SUMMARY

The basis for dysfunctional experience can now be summed up as follows: Intentions can be constrictive or expansive. The greater the discrepancy between one's intentions and one's perceived surroundings, the greater the likelihood of dysfunction. Dysfunction entails an extreme fear of the force that is perceived to oppose one. The fear is of this force's otherness, extremity, and ultimately (constrictive or expansive) infinitude or morbidity. Such fears arise in acute, chronic, and implicit contexts.

To put these principles in terms of simple advice: Don't push overly deferent people into assertive roles and overly assertive people into deferent roles. Equally, don't force highly focused people into incorporating roles, and highly incorporating people into focused roles. Finally, if you are overly deferent, focused, assertive, or incorporating, be careful about how this behavior "rubs off" on your children. It could be contagious!

Chapter Four

THE EXTREMISM OF EVERYDAY LIFE: CONVENTIONAL ANSWERS TO TERROR

Normal men have killed perhaps 100,000,000 of their fellow normal men in the last fifty years.

—R.D. Laing

We have established how immobilizing, and its reverse, chaotic, paradox can be. It is now time to look at a subtler problem: the "everyday" manifestations of these effects.

IDOLATRY

Let's face it. Despite the many benefits to conventional living, there are equally many drawbacks. There are, in fact, aberrations in the conventional mentality. And if they are not dealt with soon, they will subdue us all.

In bald terms, the greatest distinction between the

"mad" and the conventional is with respect to the management of terror. Whereas fear "blows" dysfunctional people "away," it is "buffed and polished" by the time it strikes the conventional. Conventional people find myriad gimmicks to distort, mollify, and avoid spatiotemporal extremity (see Becker, 1973; Barrett, 1978; Hoffer, 1951). Becker's (1982) discussion of the medical explanation for birth is illustrative:

> You don't know where you came from—oh, I know, you say "the sperm and the egg." Sperm and the egg! . . . Idiot answer. It's not an answer at all, it's merely a description of a speck in a causal process that is a mystery. We don't know where babies come from. You get married, you're sitting at a table having breakfast— there are two of you—and a year later there's somebody else sitting there. And if you're honest with yourself, you don't know where [he or she] came from. . . . [He or she] came, literally, out of nowhere, and [he or she] keep[s] growing in your environment. If you stop to think about it, which you don't because it's annoying, it's upsetting, then it's a total mystery. (p. 12)

The advertising industry provides us with similar examples of this sort of distortion. When a credit card company proclaims "master the possibilities,"[1] to which "possibilities" do they refer—fancy shoes, jewelry, restaurants, and nightclubs? Certainly they do not refer to the humanistic and existential implications of the term. The latter, for example, interpret "possibilities" not in terms of *things* but *qualities*, such as the capacity to love, explore, create meaning, and find purpose (May, 1969). But these humanistic qualities are not bankable to the advertising industry. They are too subtle and arduous.

[1]Mastercard Corporation.

So they must be pared down to the level of a sexy girl, racy car, or fancy suit. Only then do "possibilities" engender mass appeal. All too often, then, people take the easy route and circumvent their fears. They find all sorts of idols to help them escape. It is interesting, moreover, how tolerant people are of these replacements. We take our cheating and lying for granted. This is even more true today, as we interpose technology—drugs, media, "social engineering," and bombs—between ourselves and that which we fear.

Ironically, however, we are *very intolerant* of the people this business disturbs. We place them in "re-education camps," mental hospitals, and jails. We drug them and lecture them until they are silly. Or, if they are clever enough we permit them to be our reformers, as we shall see.

FALSE CONFRONTATIONS

Let us elaborate now on our maneuvers against constrictive and expansive terror. One of the foremost problems in our society is the preoccupation with order, rules, authorities, in short, constriction (see Becker, 1973; Laing, 1967; Schneider, 1986). Many are horrified, it appears, by associations to disarray, sloppiness, unpredictability, and ultimately chaos. Even the *prospect* of expansion repels many of us. How then do we handle these disruptions? Clearly, we do not "go psychotic" over them or preoccupy ourselves as an obsessive might. And yet in a very real sense, we let our substitutes absorb the impact, letting them manage our guilt, anxiety, elation, and impulsiveness.

Think, for example, about the degree to which we value authority in the world. Think about how religions dictate our lives. Look at how they "save" us from temptation, decision making, and "standing out." Think about the varied ways we buckle under to advertising, legal, and administrative authorities.

We have to wear the right uniforms; make our bodies look and smell a certain way; take prescribed routes to work; ride in encapsulated vehicles; speak in socially acceptable fashions; fill out forms; sign contracts; sort out papers; and sit, walk, breathe, eat, and stand in acceptable ways. Even if we are poor or exist on the "fringe," we still have to perform many of these actions, sometimes all the more vigorously to improve our status (see Goffman, 1959; Royce, 1964).

Survey all of our military personnel and equipment. This is a bulwark against disorder, penetration of the other, the alien, the unmanageable into our ranks.

Review, finally, the myriad mental health authorities, who tell us what drugs to take and how to behave "appropriately." They exhort us to calm down, blend in, and act, even if we don't feel, "stable." Fromm (1965) sums up the net effect:

> The person who is normal is often less healthy than the neurotic person in terms of human values. Often he is well adapted only at the expense of having given up his self in order to become more or less the person he believes he is expected to be. All genuine individuality and spontaneity may have been lost. (p. 160)

On the other hand, witness the people in our society who overreact the other way. These are the individuals and groups that bristle at constriction. Constriction, for them, conjures up images of entrapment, passivity, and diminishment. By contrast, these people want to fly, to tangle with great dangers and speeds. They want to "take in" and "take over." They want to order others, or extend their own horizons. Like the constrictives, however, these people want to do it the quick way, the indirect and vicarious way.

They find drugs to raise them beyond earthly sensations. They employ gurus to push them past their repressions. They ravage foods, and race cars. They hoard money, pile up erotic books, and ravish sexual partners. They adopt ornate clothing and hairstyles. They venture to far-away lands and exotic entertainments. They join wild fringe groups—gangs, cults, ecstatic religious orders. They join beauty contests, society clubs, and "in" crowds. They run and drive and jump and holler and flash their way into life (see Abramson, 1984; Lasch, 1979; Hoffer, 1951).

There is a price, however, for all of this dashing. Like the constrictives, expansives do not really integrate many of their experiences. They have no real center, no "I" to hold and digest what is discovered. All is a race. All is artifice. All is veneer and contrivance. What we have here is a grand sociocultural performance (see Goffman, 1959). People clutch at toys, games, and stage props to pretend their way through. People forget that they are people and live on armaments, maneuvers against terror.

Becker understood this very keenly. We literally "plug into" a network, he said, and all is right there, hotwired to do our bidding (Becker, 1973). The conventional person, concludes Becker (1973),

> cuts out for himself a manageable world: he throws himself into action uncritically, unthinkingly. He accepts the cultural programming that turns his nose where he's

supposed to look; he doesn't bite the world off as a giant would, but in small manageable pieces as a beaver does. He uses all kinds of techniques we call "character defenses": he learns not to expose himself; he learns not to stand out; he learns to embed himself in otherpower, both of concrete persons and of things and cultural commands; the result is that he comes to exist in the imagined infallibility of the world around him. (p. 23)

PREJUDICE

This life is split in two: what is thought reprehensible in the relations between persons is thought commendable in the relations between peoples.

—Martin Buber

Another outgrowth of our retreat from spatiotemporal terror is prejudice. For example, the constrictive among us despise any hint of expansion—the people or things we view as messy, dirty, or uncontained. These prejudices can be seen in the "white" person's distrust of the person of "color." We call such people "dirty," "cunning," "wild," and "loud" (Allport, 1979). We project onto them our own fears of the mysterious, the instinctual, the impulsive, and, ultimately, the cataclysmic (see Adorno *et al.*, 1950). It is as if the white person fears that the darker person will jump out at him and explode his clean, pure world.[2]

[2]While some authorities question whether prejudice is based on racial as opposed to value differences (e.g., Rokeach, 1960), the evidence, it seems to me, upholds the validity of both factors (see Stein, Hardyck, & Smith, 1965; Triandis, 1961; Wrightsman, 1977). Prejudice is the result of perceived constrictive or expansive racial (physical) differences as well as value differences, such as individualism vs. collectivism, materialism vs. spiritualism, and so on.

If only somebody would come right out and admit, "I'm afraid of my own responses to you—their intimations of expansiveness and everything I'm impotent about or don't understand!" If only we could level in these ways, then maybe we could begin bridging the gulf. Instead, we violate each other. We erect (or have erected) black and white toilets, drinking fountains, and housing projects to stave off the threat.

There is a flipside, although somewhat less virulent in our culture, to the above. This is the prejudice of "darker" people toward "lighter." There is some evidence to suggest that dark-skinned people fear lighter people's association to rigidity, oppression, and restriction of expressiveness (Allport, 1979). This prejudice appears to exceed even the historical basis for its expression, and conjures up, from the standpoint of paradox, images of morbid diminishment, suffocation, and obliteration.

How many other ways is prejudice poisoning our world? Christians (in certain quarters) have long despised Jews, not only for killing Jesus, but for traits they themselves lacked or could not express (Adorno *et al.*, 1950; Sartre, 1948b). For example, Jews could lend money whereas Christians were forbidden to do so. Jews would not bend to autocractic rule or principles; Christians, tragically, became the willing victims of such practices. This led some Christians to characterize Jews as "money grubbers," "hoarders," and "heretics" (Allport, 1979). Accumulating wealth and nonconformism, for some Christians, thus became associated with morbid selfishness, overthrow of the established order, and uncontrollability (Allport, 1979). Such epithets toward Jews as "dirty," "bastard," and "devil" become clearer now as they throw into cold relief the Christian

preoccupation with "purity," compliance, and sinful-
ness (see Becker, 1975; Sartre, 1948b).

For the Nazis, Jewishness prompted even grander
overcompensatory responses. Jews, for the Nazis, appeared to represent everything monstrous and alien.
They were blamed for every global ill (Becker, 1975).
Jewish sensitivity, elusiveness, defiance, intellectual curiosity, and flexibility contrasted sharply with Nazi values: discipline, order, control, precision, technology,
and physical power (see Fromm, 1973). A vignette from
Hitler's own life is illustrative here:

> So great were Hitler's anxieties about [associations to
> filth and decay] . . . so crippled was he psychically, that
> he seems to have had to develop a unique perversion to
> deal with them, to triumph over them. (Becker, 1973,
> p. 248)

Becker (1973), the author of this commentary, then
goes on to quote Waite (1971):

> Hitler gained sexual satisfaction by having a young
> woman—as much younger than he as his mother was
> younger than his father—squat over him to urinate or
> defecate on his head. (p. 234)

"This was his 'private religion,' " Becker (1973) elaborated,

> his personal transcendence of his anxiety, the hyperex-
> perience and resolution of it. This was his personal trip
> that he laid not only on the Jews and the German nation
> but directly on his mistresses. It is highly significant that
> each of them committed suicide or tried to do so. (p.
> 249)

While we can conjecture about the more general
causes of Nazi hyperrestriction (and expansion)—the

extant puritanism, the wound dealt by World War I, Germany's grave economic plight—one point strikes clear: Naziism was authoritarian, and authoritarianism, in Fromm's (1973) terms, is "sadomasochistic" (see also Adorno *et al.*, 1950). This sort of person, elaborates Fromm (1973),

> is afraid of everything that is not certain and predictable, that offers surprises which would force him to spontaneous and original reactions. . . . What is new arouses fear, suspicion, and dislike, because a spontaneous, not-routinized response would be required. (p. 291)

From the standpoint of the paradox principle, expansion in the sense that the Jews expressed it had probably been highly traumatizing to the Nazis. Just what it was that had wounded them so, however, eludes our grasp (Fromm, 1973). Could it be that these very same hate-mongers, these butchers of humanity, were once spontaneous and vulnerable, if not personally, then tacitly, perhaps far back in their ancestries? And could it be that, by dint of fate, such qualities became so utterly intolerable to them (through war or catastrophe) that they literally began to kill that which served to remind them? We need more historical information here. Yet if this were the case, then one lesson is clear: a people must never place themselves in a position of such arrant naiveté about their stature that they are unable, upon its ruin, to retain their humanity (see Hoffer, 1951).

Despite the totally unjustifiable Christian and Nazi tactics outlined above, we would be remiss to overlook the extreme factions of Judaism and other minorities. These can contribute, tragically, to the very scourge Jews have battled to eradicate (Avishai, 1985; Pearl, 1984).

The main problem I point to here is zealotry (Avishai, 1985; Buber, 1967; Pearl, 1984). The Jews are the "chosen people" echoes the Old Testament. Interrelations and particularly sexual relations with non-Jews is highly discouraged by orthodoxy. Yet despite the sound historical precedents for these strictures (e.g., tyrannical oppression, bigotry), one must ask about the *degree* of preoccupation with such a concept. One must ask about the repeated stress on segregating, distancing, and admonishing the non-Jewish world (Pearl, 1984). One must even ask about whether or not this policy is in true cadence with the biblical (in particular, talmudic) precepts. Being the so-called chosen people (an elitist and time-worn dictum it seems to me) does not *a priori* imply "segregated people." It can, as Spinoza (1955) and, later, Buber (1967) proposed, refer to the need for a learned people to assume a leadership role, a role of exchange, dialogue, and global reform. This, it would seem, is the more vital message.

Such a stand—despite its risks—is even more urgent today, as uprisings on the Palestinian front intensify. "Paradoxically," *Time* magazine (April 4, 1988) warns in terms relevant to this treatise, "Israel's moral territory has contracted as its physical space has expanded. Israel must consider the dangers of the authoritarian temptation" (p. 50).

At the same time, we cannot be naive about how difficult the latter stance remains in today's world. Hate continually begets hate, and polarization all too often remains the only realistic option. And yet if Jews (and other "out-groups") could strive, even slightly more vehemently than they have, to examine their own role in these cycles, their own resistance even to sincere gestures for exchange by the "majority" world, extremism will then have been dealt its noblest blow.

We are not too far afield when we point out that men have suppressed women with similar dogmatic, oppressive, and segregational tactics to those outlined above. The male stress on certainty, regulation, analysis, and external behavior contrasts sharply with characteristic female emphases, such as nurturance, spontaneity, affectivity, and community (Eisler, 1987; Gilligan, 1982). Nowhere does this bias sting more, perhaps, than in our "authoritative" tracts on human development. Authors, typically male, appear to exalt patriarchal values—specialization, separatism, individualism—to the neglect of equally fruitful matriarchal qualities. Gilligan (1982) elaborates:

> Among those men whose lives have served as the model for adult development, the capacity for relationships is in some sense *diminished* and the men are *constricted* in their emotional expression. Relationships often are cast in the language of achievement, characterized by their success or failure, and *impoverished* in their affective range. (p. 154, italics mine)

Our mythopoetic distinctions, moreover, bespeak similar prejudices: cities and buildings are characteristically "male," as in Carl Sandburg's "city with the big shoulders," while oceans, storms, and earthly terrain are depicted as "female." The blade and weapons of war are celebrated more fervently in many places than the chalice and instruments of peace (Eisler, 1987).

What we are now in a better position to see is that "feminine" qualities, beyond inducing sexual anxiety, associate almost graphically to everything men are trained and embodied to resist. From conception, men are commanded to narrow their space and time. "Do things right, quickly, orderly, and dispassionately," they are enjoined. "Be sensible," meaning use only your five senses, and "straighten yourself out," meaning do not act emotionally, like a woman, are also familiar male directives. Perception through the male body is similarly restrictive. Angular contours, scissor-like steps, and firm surfaces stand out in sharp relief from the fleshy, curvy female frame. Hence, it is in these disparities, these spatiotemporal opposites, that the seeds of terror take root. Femininity is not just a sexual "other" to many men, it is a personal, cultural, evolutionary, geographical, climatic, and cosmic "other" as well.

Now that we have examined some of the more "recognized" forms of bias let us look at several that receive less attention. The police, for example, who are obliged to keep our social order, are sometimes prejudiced against those who, however well intentioned, threaten to subvert that order (Wrightsman, 1977). Such prejudice seems to stem from a fear of social anarchy and displays itself in a variety of hyperconstrictive forms: "police brutality," unjustified vigilance, racial and social insensitivity, and undue suppression of dissent (see Hampden-Turner, 1970, and Fromm, 1947).

Wealthy people sometimes prejudge poorer people in a similar manner (Schlesinger, 1986). Wealth tends to bias people toward isolationism and conservatism. The poor are seen as drains on the economy, impulsive, ill-tempered, and ill-willed (Allport, 1973; Wrightsman, 1977). But worst of all, from the materialist point of view, poverty is a symbol of the disavowal of one overriding task in life: obsessiveness with "things" (Fromm, 1947).

The so-called fashionable, or beautiful, appear to have similar biases against those considered boors or homely. Fashionable people seem to have a revulsion for anything or anyone at variance with cultural tastes (Becker, 1973; Fromm, 1947). Unstylish or impoverished clothing, disfigured people, the obese, those living on the fringes or social frontiers—all are threats to the smoothness, neatness, evenness, and harmoniousness that, on a superficial level at least, pervade the fashionable world. What is "ugliness" for these people but the abrupt intrusion of the new and extravagant? What is boorishness but the heaving, teeming, urges within that threaten so to rip into fabric, make-up, and skin? What is worse for the fashionable than to be stained, soiled, or torn? What is more embarrassing than to be loud, angry, or peculiar? This is their Hitchcockian nightmare.

Another bias that bears consideration is that of the so-called intelligentsia toward the underdeveloped or "ignorant." Notice the dichotomies we create for these groups—"sharp" vs. "dull," "slick" vs. "thick," "penetrating" vs. "diffuse," "quick" vs. "slow," "bright" vs. "dim." What emerges here is the equation of intelligence with restricted surfaces—"sharp," "slick," "penetrating," and "bright." Correspondingly, "intelligent people" tend to regard more inclusive types—those who are "slower," broader, less discerning—as ignorant (Benedict, 1934; Lee, 1959). Related are people's wide variety of linguistic prejudices. Witness, for example, the bias of those who use standard English against those who use the Cockney dialect.

This problem recalls the debate between "hard" scientists and "soft" scientists. Hard scientists, such as physicists and chemists, tend to view soft scientists, such as psychologists, as imprecise, ethereal, and romantic (Giorgi, 1970; Kuhn, 1970). Hard scientists have so far "won the day" in our culture, and have legitimated only that which can be measured, quantified, and observed through the senses. Foucault (1965) outlines the historical context:

> A sensibility was born which had drawn a line and laid a cornerstone, and which chose only to banish. The concrete space of classical society reserved a neutral region, a blank page where the real life of the city was suspended; here, order no longer freely confronted disorder, reason no longer tried to make its own way among all that might evade or seek to deny it. Here reason reigned in the pure state, in a triumph arranged for it in advance over a frenzied unreason. (p. 64)
>
> The age of reason confined. (p. 65)

The age of reason confined, we might add, to bolster our affair with machines, our affair with *convenience* (Becker, 1975). Meandering thought processes foul all of this up. They splatter dirt on the print-outs, and force us to face ourselves. They compel us, finally, to ponder our rootlessness.

Conservative people in our society sometimes have similar biases toward liberals (Allport, 1979; Rokeach, 1960). "Hippies," "beatniks," and "radicals" are considered deviants. They bend sedentary rules and disrupt ordinary times. They add something new, something different to the mindscape. They are the wavy lines on our "straight" demographics. And yet it is not the isolated "blips" that disturb these conservatives so, but the *endlessness*, the *infinitude* that such blips represent.

The conservative Harry, for example, meets Tom, a long-haired drifter. Harry produces the following associations: "Drifters are wild. Wildness is upsetting. Wildness stained my suit the other day. Wildness caused me to perspire. Wildness bungled my sales pitch. Wildness spoiled my business deal. Wildness debauched my daughter. Wildness separated my father from my mother. Wildness angered my wife. Wildness killed my brother. Wildness causes disease. Wildness causes war. Wildness drives people insane. Wildness causes all-out chaos. Chaos, therefore (à la Tom), must be eliminated."

What can be seen here is that, based on one set of clothes, one glimpse of hair, and one bit of biographical information, a terrifying regress of associations emerges. This regress ranges far beyond "stereotypy," or "misconception," as Allport (1973) defines it, but waltzes into the psychological core, the scaffolding of the perpetrator's existence. That which begins as relatively trivial can soon acquire cosmic proportion and overtake every moral, political, and religious fiber one possesses. It can then brutalize one, as above, into a most formidable state of enmity.

The prejudice toward animals exemplifies a similar conventional stance. Animals are our conspicuous ancestors. They recall, perhaps more than any other presence, our deepest, darkest past. They walked among primal slime and boiling crusts. They loom large, grunting, growling, prowling. How aghast we are by their pungent smells. How daunted we are by their gnarled faces. What creeping, crawling, sinewy contours they present to us. What jagged mouths and darting eyes they can hurl. How plentiful is their hair and thick fur. How alien their fluttering antennae and slithering tentacles. How oppositional they are to our sedentary ways. We picture an ant at close range, or a housefly, and instantly recoil. Again, it is the multiplicity that is dreaded here. Again, we are caught narrowing our circle; discounting our immensity—the extension, incorporation, and eruption of life.

Thoreau (1961) comments on a similar prejudice toward "nature."

> If this world were all man, I could not stretch myself, I should lose all hope. He is constraint, she [nature] is freedom to me. He makes me wish for another world. She makes me content with this. None of the joys she supplies is subject to his rules and definitions. What he touches he taints. . . . How infinite and pure the least pleasure of which Nature is basis, compared to the congratulation of mankind! (p. 103)

And do not the constrictive among us express like views about our children (see Freud's [1963, p. 160] comparison of children to animals in our dreams)? Do they not elude us also? Do they not outdazzle and outmaneuver us? Do they not shock us with their colors and their games, their fears and their dreams (see Schachtel, 1959)? Do they not foil our plans and upset our schedules? Do they not mock our roles and explode our myths? And isn't it they who embarrass us with their will and rankle us with their curiosity (Miller, 1981)?

Until now, we have been speaking mainly about hyperconstrictive prejudices. Fanaticism, however, chooses no favorites, as Hoffer (1951) concludes, and so we presently turn to hyperexpansive prejudice.

Perhaps the signal hyperexpansive prejudice is that of the physically strong toward the weak, awkward, or disabled. Sadomasochistic groups, as we have seen, possess elements of this sort of malady. Individuals, however, can be consumed by such actions (Fromm, 1973). How many of us have known bullies who perpetrate these actions on those they consider inferior? How many of us pump iron and bloat muscles to show off and flatter ourselves? How many of us, especially today, emphasize assertion and "looking out for number one"? The meek, by contrast, are perceived as small, quiet, shy, and thin. They are viewed as old, fragile, poor, and sickly. For the aggressive, these "unfortunates" represent everything "other," and yet everything horrifyingly close. The submissive remind those who dominate not only of their own impotency, as Fromm (1973) observes, but also of their own partiality, insignificance, and, ultimately, imperceptibility. There is nothing so humiliating to a dominant type than to question his size (see Becker, 1975). "Being cut down to size," or "dressed down" is about the heaviest penalty that can be levied against one at "the top." From the standpoint of paradox, *surging* people can tolerate little *collapse*, and they will use every sort of device to insure against such an eventuality.

Excessively liberal people can be similarly disposed toward conservative, or more reserved, people. This is the prejudice of those who *incorporate* against those who *segregate* (in the terms of our model). Order, refinement, and discretion are viewed with great contempt by these liberals. Elements of this bias can be found in the so-called human potential movement, Marxism, and anarchism (Allport, 1973; Lasch, 1979; Schneider, 1986).

Such liberal extremism reached its peak in a "spiritual" commune named "Rajneeshpuram." Not only were restrictions shunned here, they were eliminated. One member put it this way:

> There's a sense of total acceptability in the groups here. Nothing is condemned. There are no limitations, no restrictions; you can take things to the extreme. Group

leaders in the West place limits on what happens in their groups because of their own limitations, their own fears. . . . Here the responsibility is Bhagwan's, so the therapist can allow things to happen; he or she can afford to take risks. (FitzGerald, 1986a, p. 83)

Bhagwan Shree Rajneesh, himself, the group's "guru," was even less compromising in his views:

[H]e criticized Gandhi . . . , socialism, and tore into orthodox Hinduism. Many years later he said he had no stake in any of these positions, "but when the entire population of the country was absorbed in these tensions . . . there seemed, even if just for fun, a necessity to create controversies." (FitzGerald, 1986a, p. 77)

In keeping with this philosophy, Rajneesh encouraged the grandest excesses among group members. Sexual orgies, drug-taking, vibrant dancing, blood-curdling groans, and lavish material comforts became institutional trademarks (FitzGerald, 1986a). "The ego has to drop. . . . The mind has to disappear for God to be" Rajneesh admonished his membership (FitzGerald, 1986a, p. 81).

But when asked about similar Rajneeshian proclamations, one disgruntled adherent put it this way:

[The guru] encouraged the letting go of one's own responsibility . . . And that's where I left. It's one thing to ask people to drop the obstructive chatter that goes on in the head and another to ask them to drop the process of discrimination. (FitzGerald, 1986a, p. 81)

Excesses such as those above soon began to exact their toll. No longer was "the establishment" an inconvenience; it became the enemy and eventually the very devil itself. Based on very little evidence, outsiders were suspected of meddling, suppressing religious freedom, and mass bigotry (FitzGerald, 1986b). Soon, factions of Rajneeshpuram's own membership became suspect, were gossiped about, spied on, and publicly condemned. And in its very last days, commune leadership allegedly resorted to the most atrocious means of defense. They began to castigate, strong arm, drug, and possibly even poison suspected dissenters (FitzGerald, 1986b). What began as a revolt against the forces of perceived oppression ended as a maniacal bulwark against that perception. We would do well here to heed the prophetic words of Eric Hoffer (1951):

> Even the mass movements which rise in the name of freedom against an oppressive order do not realize individual liberty once they start rolling. So long as the movement is engaged in a desperate struggle with the prevailing order, or must defend itself against enemies within or without, its chief preoccupation will be with unity and self-sacrifice, which require surrender of the individual's will, judgment, and advantage. (p. 36)

Thus, what we can see here is a liberalism that slipped away from itself; a revolt born not of circumstance but of a wound, which literally sundered its victims. Rajneesh rode the crest of a frustrated upper class. Not only were many of these people intolerant of their careers; they were reviled by structure (FitzGerald, 1986a). Both too innocent and too repressed, this community emerged ripe for Rajneesh's pickings. Zeal turned into imperiousness, anger into tyranny, and egalitarianism into chaos—all in the name of "freedom." Such was the hyperexpansive contagion that befell even the sturdiest among members.

INDIVIDUAL VS. COLLECTIVE INSANITY

The inevitable conclusion deriving from the above analyses is that there is really only one difference—large though it may be—between the insanity found in mental hospitals and that found in groups. The difference is that whereas individual extremists must bear their dispositions alone, collective extremists (those whom we typically call "prejudiced") can enjoy the shoulders of hundreds, thousands, even millions of people to deflect and endure their terror. I wonder what Hitler would have been like if he had not found a nation to accept his "trip." Who would Stalin have been without his acquiescent Politburo? Yet Hitler had his wounded Germany, and Stalin his vengeful Bolsheviks. We cannot underestimate the power of these collective injuries, which place *nations* as gravely at risk as individuals who are traumatized (Fromm, 1955; Hoffer, 1951). To illustrate this point, consider two very different views—one prejudiced, the other, relatively detached—of the following (hypothetical) vignette:

A rather "testy" young white boy was injured one day. The person who injured him was black. The white youth, as a result, grew up to become very contemptuous of blacks. He began separating himself from them, calling them names, and condemning them in private. He tried to enlist white support for his position by publicly denouncing blacks. He forbade his wife and children from associating with blacks, and demeaned friends who already did so. He started to feel that blackness was some kind of disease—like cancer or leprosy. He grew to be very careful about drinking, eating, or making physical contact with blacks lest he would somehow catch their "illness." He started lobbying po-

litical officials about the alleged blight and tried to orga-
nize some legal sanctions. Failing this, he started dress-
ing like a clergyman, burned large crosses, and joined a
group that lynched several black youths.

Now what is readily apparent here is that our own
culture carves out two very distinct opinions of this sort
of scenario (a not atypical one as recently as the 1960s).
One is that the white youth is insane or, at the very
least, deranged; the other is that he is virtuous and
protective of his race.

How can we blame so-called mental illness for so
much of our crime when attitudes such as the latter float
about? A little girl in a mental hospital, as Laing (1969)
points out, may believe that an atomic bomb is ticking
inside her, but millions of "regular folk" are engaged in
"holy wars" and potential "star wars" to relieve their
anxieties. A psychiatric patient may spend days clean-
ing an imaginary spot on his shirt, but thousands of
"normal" people spend *years* attempting to eliminate
other peoples' folklore, rituals, and customs.

Conventional people, then, not only have sanc-
tioners for their bigotry, but whole nations or institutions to support them. This is what makes their renun-
ciation of paradox (over and above the individual's) so
dangerous.

In conclusion, we can see that prejudice is as extreme as any individual polarization, and probably
worse, from the standpoint of planetary survival. It
should not be surprising, moreover, that such *social*
overcompensation begins very much like that regarding
the individual—with some form of trauma. Acute trauma (of which the vignette is an illustration) probably
yields its small share. Some people, for example, acquire prejudices against the poor because they have

been robbed or forcefully beaten by one of them (see Allport, 1973, p. 27, on "overgeneralization"). A similar number of cases can probably be substantiated for chronic trauma. For example, some people, appear browbeaten—by parents, friends or peers—into abhorring minorities, despite initial impressions to the contrary (Allport, 1973, p. 327).

Implicit trauma, however, may well account for the "lion's share" of prejudicial attitudes. Classic studies in the etiology of prejudice (Allport, 1979, p. 297; Rokeach, 1960,pp.159–166) indicate that prejudicial attitudes are readily emulated by many children.

SIGNS, SYMBOLS, AND DREAMS

Now that we have examined idols and mobs, let us look at other, less obvious means by which we distort terror—signs, symbols, and dreams. Recently, I attended a psychological association meeting in which a psychoanalytically oriented therapist made a very existential remark: "The worst fear in human being," he imparted, "is fear without end" (Rutan, 1987). Yes, "fear without end," I whispered to myself. This is *the* problem not only of dysfunctional behavior, as pointed out earlier, but of much that we term "civilized" humanity as well. Culture, as Becker (1975) intimates, is an *immunization* project. It is a prophylaxis against all that does not end, against all that defies us and makes a mess of things. While culture can have its proactive (actualizing) elements, ultimately, it is reactive and erected primarily to protect (Becker, 1975).

The sign, in our society, is an example par excellence of this cultural drive to localize the infinite. The sign conveys specific directions or information. We have signs for stopping, going, and yielding. We have street signs and store signs. We have insignias to dictate our status in the military, government, or clergy. We even have linguistic signs (e.g., punctuation) to tell us how to navigate our speech.

Symbols, on the other hand, are less clear. Symbols do not so much "tell" as evoke or "show" something about the world (Wittgenstein, 1961). Needleman (1975) puts it this way:

> The difference between sign and symbol, expressed phenomenologically, is that whereas the symbol expresses and partakes of that which it is a symbol, the sign. . . . does not involve the meaning structure of the signified but only refers to the signified. (pp. 81–82)

A street sign, for example, is intended to make me "stop," but it is not intended to convey the *experience* of stopping. A bright red painting, on the other hand, is intended to disclose much about this experience, and many related ones as well, such as the sense of being "trapped," "endangered," or "infuriated."

The main question here is, how are we to interpret symbolic associations? What is our organizing principle for them, and how faithful is it to the phenomenon under study?

Freud (1963) finds his answer in the area of dreams: "An overwhelming majority of symbols in dreams," he writes, "are sexual symbols" (p. 16l). Freud (1963) is brilliantly—if at times amusingly—insistent on this point:

> The male genital organ is symbolically represented in dreams in many different ways, with most of which the common idea underlying the comparison is easily ap-

parent. . . . The sacred number *three* is symbolic of the whole male genitalia. . . . The penis is symbolized primarily by objects which resemble it in form, being long and upstanding, such as *sticks, umbrellas, poles* . . . and the like . . . also by objects which, like the thing symbolized, have the property of penetrating. (pp. 161–162)

"The peculiar property of this member," Freud (1963) goes on,

being able to raise itself upright in defiance of the law of gravity . . . leads to symbolic representation by means of *balloons, aeroplanes,* and, just recently, *zeppelins.* But dreams have another, much more impressive way of symbolizing erection; they make the organ of sex into the essential part of the whole person, so that the *dreamer himself flies.* (p. 162)

After discussing the relation between male genitalia and flying, Freud (1963, p. 163) goes on to point out their similarity to reptiles, fishes, hands, and feet. He then turns to female sexual representations:

The female genitalia are symbolically represented by all such objects as share with them the property of enclosing a space or are capable of acting as receptacles: such as *pits, hollows and caves,* and also *jars and bottles,* and *boxes* of all sorts and sizes, *chests, coffers, pockets, and so forth.* (Freud, 1963, p. 163)

Ships, cupboards, stoves, rooms, gates, doors, tables, books, and shellfish are also described within this purview, as with apples, peaches, and fruit for women's breasts (Freud, 1963, p. 163). Although Freud (1963) goes on to describe "birth," "death," and "earth" representations, he does not stray from sexuality. These too, he declares, relate to maternal and vaginal themes (Freud, 1963), or the pleasure and unpleasure of childhood sensations (Needleman, 1975).

Now there are two basic criticisms here: First, Freudian symbolism is unnecessarily delimited. Concrete elements, for example, knives, are associated to other concrete elements, for example, penises. Nowhere is the question asked, "What do the penises represent?"(see Binswanger, 1975; Jaspers, 1963). Sexual symbolism ends the investigation. Binswanger (1975), for example, finds that "hoarding" relates to more than just the reminiscence of "retaining one's feces," but to a sense of emptiness and the need to fill it.

For Jaspers symbols are partial and indefinite. The best they can do is to capture relevant *themes*, not "hardened" knowledge:

> To live deeply rooted in symbols is to live in a reality which as yet we do not know but can appreciate in symbolic form. Symbols, therefore, are infinite, accessible to infinite interpretation and inexhaustible, but they are never the reality itself as an object which we could know and possess. (Quoted in Corrington, 1987, pp. 73–74)

Fixating symbols, Jaspers goes on, poses the danger of gross inaccuracy:

> Where historical and psychological knowledge is treated as if it could provide effective symbols for suffering people, superstition may be the result, a credulous belief which attempts in a limited fashion to fixate symbols that are themselves indefinite, constantly in motion and not to be grasped objectively. (Quoted in Corrington, 1987, p. 74)

A second problem with psychoanalytic symbolism is its overemphasis on the past (Binswanger, 1975; Klein, 1976). Manifest content, for all practical purposes, is dismissed. Only that which is remote and hidden is legitimated. The "real" underlying issues are thought to be infantile and may have little to do with the patient's *current* and *potential* concerns. Yet there simply is no empirical justification for such a "latent" orientation, especially with regard to dream symbolism (Fisher & Greenberg, 1985; Krippner & Dillard, 1988).

Heidegger made this point also. Craig (1988) paraphrases: "[T]here [is a] hidden meaningfulness. . . . [But] this . . . meaning [is] not *other* than what appears but rather precisely and only what constitutes the very thing that is trying to reveal itself" (p. 10).

Although Jung (1966)—and, later, object-relation theorists (Guntrip, 1969)—broadened the psychoanalytic framework, they are not exempt from our critique.

Jung (1974), for example, who accused Freud of restrictive dream interpretations, failed to see his own delimiting practices. Specifically, I point to Jung's stress on the mythic aspects of symbolism to the neglect of experiential elements (Binswanger, 1975; Jaspers, 1963). Not only do these mythic interpretations stop short of what would appear to be a fuller, spatiotemporal understanding; they fail, in some cases, to grasp what is *essential* in a patient's experience (May, 1958b). One patient, for example, complained that a pivotal dream he had about being suspended in a church tower was misinterpreted by his Jungian analyst. The analyst apparently dwelled on the dream's archetypal significance and neglected its immediate implications. The patient did not improve, reportedly, until he was able to move beyond intellectual discussions about archetypes and confront his dream in a bodily, experiential way (Boss cited in May, 1958b, p. 53).

Object-relation theorists also truncate the patient's moment to moment *situation*. For them, symbolism is traced to separation from the caretaker (Guntrip, 1969).

No matter when or where someone is disturbed, separation concerns are focused upon in treatment (Guntrip, 1969).

It may be more fruitful, accordingly, to view dreams, not as historical byproducts, but as "metaphors" for current problems (Krippner & Dillard, 1988; Fisher & Greenberg, 1985). What is the anxious "core" of the dream, we might ask (Krippner & Dillard, 1988). In what ways does it resonate with present concerns? When dreamers respond to such questions, sexual, mythic, and separation themes tend to be of only partial significance (Krippner & Dillard, 1988). Of more import, frequently, are the global "incongruities" (or "paradoxes" as I would term them) between constrictive and expansive tendencies (see Krippner & Dillard, 1988, p. 106). Hence, not only sexual, mythic, and separation themes seem to be integral to dreamers' lives, but a wide range of spatiotemporal issues as well. Witness, for example, the following:

Hannah dreamed she was driving up a hill in a police car. There was a ceiling at the top of the hill and she felt it marked the limits to how far she could go. Suddenly, her car turned into a rocket ship and blasted through the ceiling into space. (Krippner & Dillard, 1988, p. 113)

How are we to interpret this sequence? Let us consider our several methods. The psychoanalyst might view the dream in sexual terms—e.g., Hannah wishes to have a penis ("rocket ship") so that she can dominate or compete with men. The Jungian might view it in mythic terms—e.g., Hannah is a repressed "warrior" who must "blast through" an enemy force. The object-relation therapist might view it in separation-attachment terms—e.g., Hannah wishes to separate ("blast" away) from her intrusive parents. The existential therapist, finally, might view it in terms of the paradox principle—e.g., Hannah struggles to counter (expand) some current experience of oppression (constriction). That the latter may be the most useful interpretation is borne out by Hannah herself. She concluded that

> the police car represented her carefully regimented life in which she obeyed all the traditional "rules." The ceiling was a self-imposed limit, but one she could break through if she altered her vehicle, that is, if she broke some of the rules which may no longer have applied to her. (Krippner & Dillard, 1988, p. 113)

The evolutionist Charles Darwin was alleged to have a similar "night-terror": "Someone," he reportedly dreamt, "had been executed first by hanging and then by decapitation. Somehow the character survived, 'having faced death like a hero'" (Krippner & Dillard, 1988, p. 105).

While the psychoanalyst might point to castration anxiety, the Jungian to an ancient "odyssey," and the object-relation therapist to childhood separation issues, the existentialist would probably explore Darwin's sense of prevailing (expanding) despite being (constrictively) "choked," and "cut down" in his life. Again, the latter view, report Krippner & Dillard (1988), appears to be the most serviceable:

> This dream has been interpreted metaphorically to reflect Darwin's awareness that he was approaching a revolutionary idea that would initially subject him to harsh criticism but ultimately to praise and renown. The double aspect of the execution also could have been a meta-

phor: the dream took place at the time of his impending marriage—a commitment he may have thought would supersede the time he could devote to science. (p. 105)

"Being 'like a hero,'" the authors conclude, may reflect Darwin's desire (and subsequent ability) to expansively face his harsh critics while at the same time supporting a family.

"Nanhoi," as Krippner & Dillard (1988, pp. 111–112) call him, appears to have had a dream about overexpansion. Specifically, he dreamed about a king who is seized by archers and held for ransom. They demand that he give them either his kingdom or his treasury. Assuming that he has no gold left in his palace, the king prepares to relinquish his rule. At that moment, however, several subjects realize that he has gold hidden in a cast on his leg. He, in turn, realizes that more gold is hidden in unexpected places in the palace (e.g., in furniture), and the archers permit him to continue ruling his kingdom.

Now what Nanhoi discovered here, the authors report, was not peculiarly sexual, mythical, or objectrelational but starkly lived: Nanhoi had been a greedy businessman most of his life and it was time, he realized, for a shift in priorities (Krippner & Dillard, 1988). It was time for him to *retract* from his harried and superficial ways and *yield* to a more "mundane" yet caring path (Krippner & Dillard, 1988, p. 112). Nanhoi's dream was emphatic on this point. Recall that once the king began to recognize his "inner" riches (e.g., the "gold" in the dream), the archers lost their greed. They realized (as did Nanhoi upon awakening) that the "treasure was not all in one place but in everything around" them, "if" they "could only take the time to" share and "appreciate it" (Krippner & Dillard, 1988, pp. 112-113).

The plea elucidated by these vignettes, then, is for a *relevant* understanding of symbols. This means an acknowledgment of the spatiotemporal, as opposed to an isolated historical basis for one's perception, and the endlessness or infinitude which attends. It means that one's fear of greed, guns, penises, archers, or any other *inclusive* force may relate to a multitude of associations, many of which center on unchecked expansion, dispersion, and ultimately chaos. A dream, a wish, an image—each could reactivate this dread. Each is a hologram of the larger fear.

The fear of being trapped, abused, demeaned, correspondingly, may relate to a sense of constricting, dissipating, and finally vanishing, as Hannah and Darwin may well have apprehended. Submission, entrapment, fragility, impotency, and abandonment associations may also produce such concerns (see Becker, 1973). Let me be clear that I am speaking about a sense of more than just "shrinking" or "sinking," to use Binswanger's (1975) terms, but a sense of *eternal* diminishment.

The reasons for the exaggerations, magnifications, intensifications and the like of dreams, altered states, and psychoses should be clearer now: *every* experience is exaggerated and intensified in its fuller context. The question is, how much and to what extent does one pursue this context? To what extent is one "overtaken" by it?

Another source of data that is relevant to this question is the Rorschach Test. This test is especially useful because, unlike structured instruments, it is relatively ambiguous and rich in potential symbolism. This ambiguity, writes Schachtel (1966, p. 23), "offers . . . countless *possibilities* of perceiving. . . . [It] confront[s] the testee with a freedom of choice and with the predicament of this very freedom."

Now if the paradox principle is to have weight in the present context, then spatiotemporal (constrictive /expansive) themes, as opposed to isolated sexual, mythical, or "separation" themes, should punctuate Rorschach protocols. Furthermore, to the degree that dysfunction increases, spatiotemporal production should also intensify on these tests.

That this, indeed, is the case is illustrated by the stress testees (and scorers) place on the *contours* (forms, colors, movements) in Rorschach protocols, as opposed to circumscribed content areas. The greater the testee's dysfunction, moreover, the more pronounced this emphasis. Schachtel (1966) elaborates:

> I am convinced that it is misleading to assume that any specific content can be assigned to any particular card. . . . Instead, it is more fruitful to examine the distinctive perceptual qualities of the various blots and significant and typical reactions to these qualities. (pp. 32–33)

He goes on,

> The structural and other perceptual qualities in which the various inkblots differ from each other are best described by arranging them around certain *perceptual themes* each of which, in turn, may be thought of as extending between two opposite poles. (p. 33)

Schachtel (1966, p. 29) describes these poles in terms of "balance and imbalance," "symmetry and asymmetry." He then goes on to describe their specific qualities, each of which can be understood on the basis of constriction and expansion:

> They may be designated as directedness versus diffusion; focused or unfocused; smoothness, evenness versus raggedness, jaggedness; fluid versus angular lines; openness versus closedness; shelter versus oppression;

pointedness versus roundedness; completeness versus
incompleteness; viable space and freedom to move versus crowdedness and collision. (p. 41)

These polarities become more vivid, Schafer (1948)
shows, as dysfunction increases: "When rigidity in any
one or several respects becomes pronounced or when
controls appear ineffective, a neurosis is suggested"
(p. 96).

Schizophrenics can oscillate to an even greater degree. Wagner (1981) reports that they

can be intensely preoccupied with each percept, ex-
pounding, detailing, and fabulizing the images as if
they were real, or they can dart from one percept to
another, pressured by an obsessive flow of ideas. (p. 67)

Schafer (1948) summarizes these points:

The "objective" reality of the testing situation and the
inkblot is taken neither too seriously nor too lightly by
the normal subject. If it is taken too seriously, we can
describe the subject's thinking as having *lost distance*
from the card; if it is taken too lightly, the thinking
shows an *increase of distance*. . . . In many schizophrenic
responses both loss and increase of distance can be seen
in simultaneous operation. (p. 71)

It can now be understood how content areas warp
"in and out" spatiotemporally. Schizophrenic content is
"bizarre," "otherworldly," and "cosmic" (Exner, 1986;
Wagner, 1981). It is obsessed, not with genitals, parents, or archaic rituals *per se*, but with "forces," "rays,"
and "creatures" (Wagner, 1981, pp. 56 & 68). When
areas such as sexuality are referred to by schizophrenics, they are likely to be given to "many tiny pro-
jections, invaginations, or confluences" (Schafer, 1948,

p. 70). They are often "gory ('inflamed foreskin of a penis'), confabulated ('two women with their vaginas together') or colored by blunted affect ('this one would be too loose'—speaking of a vagina)." They also may be highly contradictory: "A single confabulated or otherwise strange or vivid sex response in a very constricted record may . . . be diagnostic [of schizophrenia]" (Schafer, 1948, p. 70).

Body parts and relationships are also referred to in exaggerated forms. Body parts, for example, may be seen as skeletal structures, X-rays, and withered skins (Wagner, 1981). They may be depicted by "contaminations," or the fusion of widely disparate elements. "Bug/ox," "butter/flower," and "sparrow-flying-eagle-moth," as one of my former clients put it, are illustrative (Exner, 1986; Wagner, 1981).

Relationships are likely to be portrayed with equal fluidity. "When I first looked at these [blots]," one woman uttered, "they looked like doctors in surgical outfits in conference. The more I look at it, they look like men in uniform. They work in another planet—not here—or in the future" (Schafer, 1948, p. 252).

Jaspers (1963) notes that schizophrenic art can also suggest this "urgency to present some . . . world-picture" and penetrate "to the essence of things" (p. 292). He takes an interest in the "*form*" of their creations as well, and finds in it

> a certain pedantry, exactness, laboriousness; a striving for violent effects; stereotyped curves; making everything in a circle; or there are angular lines. . . . When we try to understand the effect of the drawings on their author . . . we find the simplest thing is symbolically important and a rich fantasy [is] woven around it. (Jaspers, 1963, p. 292)

What can be seen through these portrayals is that it is not so much sexual, mythic, or object-relational content that grips one about symbol formation, but the exaggerations, extrapolations, or, in short, *configurations* of those modalities (see Klein, 1976; Shapiro, 1965). Psychotic experience—and quite probably the horizons of ordinary experience—appears to draw its energy from sources other than cultural or even planetary domains. The further out we get the less we dwell on what is delimited by the culture, and the more we involve ourselves with the infinitude of those standpoints. This is why oscillating reaction times, disarrayed or razor sharp forms (thoughts), unbounded or absent colors (feelings), and frenzied or paralyzed movements (active/passive ideas) on projective tests are so telling (Exner, 1986; Jaspers, 1963; Schachtel, 1966; Wagner, 1981). They express the degree of one's "shock" toward this world, and one's trajectory opposing that shock.

To sum up, signs are the conventional means of arranging constrictive and expansive terror. Symbols are the personal means of doing so. Freudians, Jungians, and object-relation theorists move closer to this understanding but cut it prematurely short. They fail to heed Becker's (1973) observation that it is not this or that conflict, but "life" that is the problem. They fail to see that it is not reminiscences that are at stake here, not faulty childhood internalizations; but the endlessness, the spatiotemporal *forms* of those and similar experiences that are so jarring. To the degree that we are exposed to those forms, as appears to be the case in dreams, projective tests, and art, we tend to become uneasy, and yet can learn a great deal about ourselves. To the degree that we can no longer tolerate or control that exposure, however, we become dysfunctional or, in dire cases, psychotic.

The farther reaches of consciousness, finally, cannot be fully grasped by what is old, played out, or presupposed, but by that which also encompasses the fresh, novel, and possible. This is the message of clinical data, and of William Blake:

> To see a world in a grain of sand
> And a heaven in a wild flower
> To hold infinity in the palm of your hand
> And eternity in an hour

Chapter Five

OPTIMAL CONFRONTATIONS WITH PARADOX

In creative activity, genius is at the ultimate limit of tension, the utmost reach, of intensity, penetration. . . . But no wonder it overtakes the physical and mental powers, and unbalances the high-strung genius.

—Radoslav Tsanoff

We have now examined two responses to infinitude: the dysfunctional and the conventional. Dysfunctional people tend to directly and conventional people indirectly evade constrictive or expansive terror. Dysfunctional people tend to find *personal* means to escape their dread, such as schizophrenia, depression, and a rich world of symbols. Conventional people tend to find *less* personal means to escape, such as drugs, prejudices, religions, and a wide asssortment of signs.

Yet what would it be like if people had a different response to infinitude? What would it be like if people were motivated by more than just terror, but by liberal doses of interest, attraction, and fascination? What if people dared to grapple with their polarities and maintained some sense of control over them? What would these people be like individually? What would they be like collectively? Despite our sparse knowledge in these areas, a profile of such people does appear to be emerging (see, for example, Becker, 1973; Bellah *et al.*, 1985; Garfield, 1986; Gilligan, 1982; Kobasa, 1979; Linville, 1987; Maslow, 1968; May, 1969; Schachtel, 1959).

In particular, it appears that such people are "healthier," or what existentialists call more integrated, creative, or hardy, than ordinary people. This does not mean that life is geometrically balanced for them or that they practice "moderation in all things," as the Greeks admonished. Far from it. It means, however, that optimal people—especially within the limited sphere of their interests—dare to challenge and confront their constrictive and expansive capacities. They find the "right" (that is, most useful)[1] blend of constriction and expansion to meet relevant demands (see Rothenberg, 1979).

As a result, optimal people show relatively fewer debilitating symptoms and conflicts, especially in their areas of expertise (Maslow, 1968; Linville, 1987). They have a greater sense of personal and collective purpose (see Bellah *et al.*, 1985; Garfield, 1986; Kobasa, 1979).

---

[1]The concept of optimal functioning, like the paradox principle, rests on radical empiricist (James, 1963), and pragmatic grounds (Rorty, 1979). Radical empiricism purports that not only sense perception and the intellect are legitimate areas for scientific inquiry, but *any* human faculty, including the imagination, intuition, and emotions. Pragmatism asserts that the final arbiter of these perspectives is not metaphysical (or meta-communal), but the force of individual and collective argumentation, persuasiveness, and interest. While such criteria have sometimes proven problematic for humanity, appeals to metaphysics and deities, I would argue, have proven all the more debilitating (see Giorgi, 1970; James, 1963; Kuhn, 1970; Rorty, 1979; Schlesinger, 1986; Schneider, 1989).

They tend to work harder and love more intensely (Garfield, 1986; Fromm, 1956). They enjoy the *escalation* of tension, excitement, and suspense as much or more than they do the fulfillment or outcome of such dispositions (Klein, 1976; May, 1977; Schachtel, 1959). They tend to be challenged rather than terrified by constrictive and expansive extremes, and as a result, constructively reframe those extremes (Barron, 1963; Garfield, 1986; Kierkegaard, 1954). At the same time, they sense when to retreat and "gather their forces" (Kobasa, 1979). In short, optimal people have well-developed centers—they are more able to *choose* their retractions and expansions, whereas dysfunctional and conventional people are greatly diminished in this capacity.

Arieti (1976, pp. 93–94) recapitulates:

> The endlessness of man can now be recognized. . . . Because of his challenging and transcending ways, man is a product not simply of nature but also of his own making. . . . He is no longer satisfied with the possible and the conditional; he now conceives of the impossible, the unconditional, the infinitely bigger and the infinitely smaller, the absolute, the whole, nothingness, the real, the unreal, and the unceasing expansion of reality. These functions, present in every human being, are particularly pronounced in the creative person.

EMPIRICAL STUDIES OF OPTIMAL INTEGRATION

Life consists of struggles to reach higher stages of integration within a basically irreconcilable conflict.
                                        —Bruno Bettelheim

To this point we have spoken in generalities about optimal experiences and lifestyles. Let us look now at several specific areas in which optimal functioning has been displayed and researched. Particularly, we will examine the impact of optimal integration on personality, physical health, business organization, society, and development.

OPTIMAL PERSONALITY: A STUDY IN CONTROLLED MADNESS

Empirical studies of "healthier" people have reached a rather startling conclusion: they are a lot like those who are considered mad, at least in an initial sense (Arieti, 1976; Barron, 1963; Eisenstadt, 1978; Maslow, 1968; May, 1969; Prentky, 1979).

Both optimal people and the mad, for example, tend to perceive constrictive and expansive extremes (see the illustration on p. 143) (Barron, 1963; Kris, 1952; Rank, 1936; Schachtel, 1966). For instance, Einstein combined the widest ranging cosmic insights with that of precision mathematics. Shakespeare produced incisive yet brilliantly comprehensive literary works. Freud, according to Jones (1981),

> was beyond doubt someone whose instincts were far more powerful than those of the average man, but whose repressions were even more potent. The combination brought an inner intensity of a degree that is perhaps the essential feature of any great genius. (p. 138)

Creativity research conducted at the University of California concurs:

> Creative individuals are more able than most to give expression to opposite sides of their nature, to achieve a

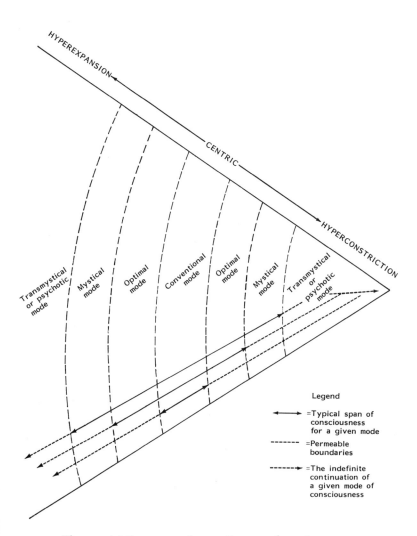

The constrictive–expansive continuum of consiousness

reconciliation of the conscious and unconscious, reason and passion, rational and irrational, science and art. All the highly creative male groups studied, for example, scored high on a "femininity" test: more open in their feelings and emotions, more sensitively aware of themselves and others, and possessing wide-ranging interests—traits which in our culture are considered "feminine." On the other hand, most of them were not effeminate in manner or appearance, but instead assertive, dominant, and self-confident. (Carnegie Corporation Staff, 1961, p. 3)

Finally, all of this squares with Maslow's (1968) studies of "self-actualizing" people:

One observation that I made has puzzled me for many years but it begins to fall into place now. It was what I described as the resolution of dichotomies in self-actualizing people. . . . These most mature of all people were also strongly childlike. These same people, the strongest egos ever described and the most definitely individual, were also precisely the ones who could be most easily ego-less, self-transcending and problem centered. (p. 140).

It is no wonder that Maslow (1968,p. 177) characterized such people as the best obsessionals and hysterics combined!

Although it has not been made very explicit by personality researchers, most (if not all) of the major diagnostic syndromes appear to be an integral part of optimal functioning. For example, marked traces of antisocial personality, impulsiveness, paranoia, anxiety, and depression could well have sparked the extravagant yet persuasive political treatises of Winston Churchill, John Stuart Mill, Mohandas Gandhi, Abraham Lincoln, and, indeed, the writers of the U.S. Constitution (see Erikson, 1975; Fieve, 1975; Schlesinger, 1986; Tsanoff, 1949).

Suicidal depression and manic qualities appear to have significantly influenced poets Robert Lowell, Anne Sexton, and Sylvia Plath, psychologist William James, philosophers Arthur Schopenhauer and Søren Kierkegaard, musician George Handel, and writers Franz Kafka, Virginia Woolf, and Eugene O'Neill (see Grant, 1968; Leo, 1984; May, 1969).

Schizoid, histrionic, and epileptic traits appear to have characterized the lives and works of Nietzsche, Van Gogh, Beethoven, Michelangelo, Byron, and Heine (see Lange-Eichbaum, 1932; Grant, 1968; Kaufmann, 1968).

Obsessive-compulsive meticulousness seems to be a key factor in the scientific observations of W. Roentgen, Tycho Brache, E.O. Lawrence, and J.R. Oppenheimer (Johnston, 1967; Kuhn, 1970, Prentky, 1979). This disposition was given a lively catch-phrase by Alfred North Whitehead, who called it "simpleminded" and humorously contrasted it with his own "muddle-minded" style (Barrett, 1978). Similarly, William James characterized such thinkers as the linear, empirically restrictive "tough-minded," in opposition to the emotionally and intuitively inclined "tenderminded" (James, 1963).

Schizophrenia, finally, has been implicated in the life and works of Strindberg, Blake, and Kafka (Grant, 1968; May, 1969). Norma MacDonald (1979), a former psychiatric in-patient, ponders this implication:

> I began to see that in schizophrenia I had much more than a handicap—I had a tool and a potential. This sort of mind, controlled and used, has a far-reaching imaginative power, a sharp instinctual awareness, and the

ability to understand a wide span of emotional and intellectual experiences. (pp. 112–113)

A second similarity between optimal people and
the mad is the *authenticity* of their encounters. Both tend
to directly, as opposed to artificially (or vicariously),
confront paradox (Eisenstadt, 1978). Both see, moreover, how artificiality restricts their possibilities for a
fuller, richer life (Arietti, 1976; Becker, 1973; May, 1969;
Prentky, 1979; Rank, 1968). "Whatever is achieved,"
writes Becker (1973) of optimal people, is "achieved
from within the subjective energies of creatures, . . .
without deadening, with full exercise of passion, of vision, of pain, of fear, and of sorrow" (p. 284).

In what would appear to be one of Thoreau's (1961)
more alienated moments, he dramatizes Becker's contention:

> All the community may scream because one man is born
> who will not do as it does, who will not conform be-
> cause conformity to him is death—he is so constituted.
> They know nothing about his case; they are fools when
> they presume to advise him. The man of genius knows
> what he is aiming at; nobody else knows. (p. 204)

To sum up: So-called psychiatric disorder is clearly
much more complex and sublime than our century has
acknowledged. While psychiatric patients may suffer
unbearable extremes, our geniuses (who flirt with similar anguish) somehow find the resources to harness and
cultivate those extremes (Farson, 1974). It would be-
hoove social scientists to tread much more cautiously in
the area of "psychopathology" and begin to look at its
redemptive as well as its degenerative implications
(Richards, 1981; Sass, 1987).

If genius and madness sharply overlap, their points
of departure, as we have suggested, are equally acute.

Whereas the mad "cave in" under the weight of their extremes, the optimal are somehow able to redirect and mobilize themselves (Eisenstadt, 1978; May, 1977). Prentky (1979) explains:

> The apparent difference between the divergent thinking, loose associations, and irrelevant themes of psychotics and the amazing conceptual leaps, cognitive flexibility, and serendipitous discoveries of creative artists and scientists is one of control. Psychotic thinking is unbridled and capricious, while creative thinking is rationally directed and purposeful. (pp. 10–11)

Architecture critic Robert Campbell (1988) elucidates a similar thought:

> You can't be creative if you don't have constraints. Creativity without constraints is like moving chess pieces around on your living room floor. You might come up with a lot of moves, but in the absence of the chessboard, they wouldn't be anything you could possibly call creative. (p. B-10)

Barron (1963), finally, provides an eloquent summary of these views:

> The decision in favor of complexity, at its best makes for originality, creativeness, a greater tolerance for unusual ideas and formulations. The sometimes disordered and unstable world has its counterpart in the person's inner discord, but the crucial ameliorative factor is a constant effort to integrate the inner and outer complexity in a higher-order synthesis. The goal is to achieve the psychological analogue of mathematical elegance: to allow into the perceptual system the greatest possible richness of experience, while yet finding in this complexity some overall pattern. Such a person is not immobilized by anxiety in the face of great uncertainty, but is at once perturbed and challenged. (p. 199)

Despite Vincent Van Gogh's allegedly tempestuous life, his *art* accords powerfully with Barron's thesis. Far from his self-destructive broods, Van Gogh's paintings reveal an unparalleled eloquence. His dazzling colors and soaring imagination combine masterfully with a fine eye for detail and thick, bold strokes. In Van Gogh's works we witness the very epitome of what May (1985, p. 34) terms the wedding of "vitality" and "form" or what I call "the integration of constrictive and expansive polarities." Van Gogh, too, observes these blends in his work. He states that the purpose of his painting is

> to express the love of two lovers by the marriage of two complementaries, their blending and oppositions, the mysterious vibrations of kindred tones. To express the thought of a brow by the radiance of a light tone on a somber background. To express hope by some star, the ardor of being by the radiance of a setting sun (quoted in Graetz, 1963, pp. 69–71)

The confrontation with and subsequent mastery of oppositions was also a hallmark of Henry David Thoreau's (1961) life. When he was in the woods, he could spot the subtlest leaf markings or catalogue an endless parade of insects. When he removed himself to his cabin, his mind could spin the loftiest philosophical webs and the boldest political commentaries. He was at "home" with both solitude and conversation, ascetic restraint and civic protest. He lived with scarcity but he enjoyed abundance. "My themes shall not be far-fetched," he writes in one of his journals. "I will tell of homely every-day phenomena and adventures."

> What you call barenness and poverty is to me simplicity. God could not be unkind to me if he should try. I love

the winter, with its imprisonment and its cold, for it
compels the prisoner to try new fields and resources.
. . . I love best to have each thing in its season only, and
enjoy doing without it at all other times. . . . I find it
invariably true, the poorer I am, the richer I am. (p. 168)

One is reminded of Goethe's reflection:

To live within limits, to want one thing, or a very few
things, very much and love them dearly, cling to them,
survey them from every angle, become one with them—
that is what makes the poet, the artist, the human
being. (Quoted in Richardson, 1986, p. xi)

The firm but temperate actions of Martin Luther
King are also illustrative of an optimal outlook. While
cities burned and bodies clashed during the black civil
rights struggle, King pursued a unique strategy.
Whereas other civil rights leaders preached violence or
passive resignation, King taught nonviolent protest.
This alternative was aimed *between* the two extremes but
nevertheless managed to capture the hopes and interests of both factions. In his "Letter from Birmingham
jail," armed with ragged scraps of paper, King proceeds
to document this strategy and convey it to a skeptical
party:

You speak of our activity in Birmingham as extreme. At
first I was rather disappointed that fellow clergymen
would see my nonviolent efforts as those of an extrem-
ist. I began thinking about the fact that I stand in the
middle of two opposing forces in the Negro community.
One is a force of complacency, made up in part of
Negroes who, as a result of long years of oppression,
are so drained of self-respect, and a sense of "somebodi-
ness" that they have adjusted to segregation. . . . The
other force is one of bitterness and hatred, and it comes
perilously close to advocating violence.

I have tried to stand between these two forces, saying
that we need emulate neither the "do-nothingism" of
the complacent nor the hatred and despair of the black
nationalist. For there is the more excellent way of love
and nonviolent protest. (King, 1969, p. 564)

Bruno Bettelheim (1960), finally, discusses the need
for similar integrations as a prisoner in a Nazi concentration camp. The question for *some* of these pris-
oners (i.e., the few who were not victims of totally ran-
dom attacks), Bettelheim reports, was one of *survival*. It
was a question of doing what one *had* to do. Those who
could not go hungry for periods, or tolerate beatings, or
control their impulses, or even kill, if necessary, would
not survive. Those who could manage these contrasts
and contradictions had a reasonably better chance. One
had to sense, Bettelheim (1960) contends, when to trust
and when to withdraw, when to speak and when to
remain silent, when to think and when to act, to main-
tain even a morsel of one's dignity and desire to live.
The problems of choice and (constrictive/expansive)
flexibility, as one veteran prisoner indicated, were of
utmost concern. "What was implied," Bettelheim (1960)
elaborates,

> was the necessity . . . to carve out, against the greatest
> of odds, some areas of freedom of action and freedom of
> thought, however insignificant. The two freedoms, of
> activity and passivity, constitute our two most basic hu-
> man attitudes, while intake and elimination, mental ac-
> tivity and rest, make up our most basic physiological
> activities. To have some small token experiences of
> being active and passive, each on one's own, and in
> mind as well as body—this, much more than the utility
> of any one such activity, was what enabled me and oth-
> ers like me to survive. (p. 148)

Summarizing the findings on optimal personality then: such people have a keen sense of proportion. They know when and in what degree to yield, focus, assert, and incorporate. There is nothing definitive or measurable about this proportion. There is no "golden mean" or perfect balance that they obtain. There is simply integration—a courageous reckoning with the infinity of choices before one. The criterion for the "truth" or validity of this integration rests, in accordance with the paradox principle, with the participants and persons affected (see note 1). Have the parties involved confronted (personal, social, transcendent) constrictive and expansive potentialities to the degree they are capable? Is their action a (personally and socially) *useful* synthesis of this confrontation? In short, has the wider context of an argument, question, or endeavor been optimally engaged? This is the best criterion for validity that human beings seem capable of constructing.

Now that we have established a link between paradox and optimal personality, let us turn to the data on paradox and physical well-being.

OPTIMAL PHYSICAL HEALTH

We already know a great deal personally about the connection between our minds and our bodies. What is the toll on our bodies, for example, when we feel frightened ("frozen," "breathless"), sad ("choked up"), obsessed (tightly "wound"), or sedentary ("flat") for long periods? By the same token, what happens to our bodies when we feel chronically rushed ("pressed"), aggressive ("forced"), aroused ("charged"), or angered ("explosive")?

Many of us know the answer intimately: we often become physically ill following such episodes. We feel invigorated, by contrast, when our energy is expressed more "proportionally." But what about the research on such experiences? What do we know experimentally? Interestingly, we now know a modest but increasing amount experimentally. This data, moreover, appears favorable not only to our "naturalistic" observations but also to the paradox principle, which is our working model for them.

Specifically, experiments show that psychological (constrictive/expansive) extremes—such as depression, anxiety, dominance, and hostility—have deleterious physical effects (Friedman & Booth-Kewley, 1987).[2] Integrative perceptions, on the other hand, appear to enhance bodily health (see Antonovsky, 1979; Kobasa, 1979).

For example, Kobasa, Maddi, and Puccetti (1982) found that psychologically "hardy" individuals (i.e., those who emphasize commitment, control, and challenge in their lives) show a remarkable immunity to physical disease. Further, those who are both hardy and exercise show an even greater physiological re-

---

[2]This hypothesis appears to have greatest validity among attitudes which may be classified as nonpsychotic. In the psychotic realm, the evidence is less clear. While manic-depressives appear to undergo significantly more cardiovascular disorders than the general population (Coleman, 1976), the extent to which psychotropic drugs play a role confounds this picture (Ghadirian & Engelsmann, 1985). Likewise, although schizophrenics appear to suffer from a host of neurologically related disorders and early death, there is also an indication that they may be resistant to certain physical disorders, such as heart disease and cancer (Ghadirian & Engelsmann, 1985). The research is simply too premature in this area to draw any firm conclusions (Ghadirian & Engelsmann, 1985).

silience (Kobasa, Maddi, & Puccetti, 1982). These authors conclude that those who are "open" yet find a sense of purpose and control, as well as exercise, may decrease physiological strain.

Linville (1987), in a study of self-complexity, relates a similar finding. The more people can identify with divergent (especially *highly* divergent) aspects of themselves (e.g., "good tennis player," "lover of music"), she reports, the more resistant they are to stress and certain physical illnesses (Linville, 1987).

Antonovsky (1979), finally, reports that individuals who attain a "cohesive," organized sense of self are physically more resilient than those who are polarized or fragmented psychologically (p. 10).

Regarding perceptual extremes, Friedman and Rosenman (1974) found that "Type A" persons (or those who emphasize speed, impatience, and competition) are at greater risk for coronary heart disease than "Type B" people, who do not emphasize these qualities. Kobasa, Maddi, and Zola (1983), on the other hand, found that psychological hardiness has a moderating effect on the Type A personality. Those who were found low in hardiness reported more general illness than those who were found high in hardiness. This suggests that "control," "commitment," and "openness" may beneficially moderate Type A traits.

More recent research indicates that the Type A-disease connection is not as clear as once thought. However, the Type A personality in combination with hostility (both intra- and extrapunitive) has been found to be salient (Williams, 1984; Wood, 1986).

Loneliness and affiliation have been further linked to physiology. Widowers, in one study, had a 40% greater death rate than the normal population for their

age group within the first six months of the death of
their spouses (Parks, Benjamin, & Fitzgerald, 1969). Another study showed positive immune system changes
for subjects rated high on love and affiliation (McClelland, cited in Ornstein and Sobel, 1987).

High needs for power and dominance, conversely,
have shown adverse physiological effects. McClelland,
Ross, and Patel (1985) found that subjects with high and
frustrated power needs show negative immune system
changes. Elevated extraversion ratings may be related
to an increased risk of coronary heart disease and head-
aches (Friedman and Booth-Kewley, 1987).

Research in the areas of depression, pessimism,
and anxiety is also beginning to show a physiological
connection. For example, Goodkin, Antoni, and Blaney
(1986) found that pessimism and anxious attitudes toward life are associated with an increased risk for pre-
cancerous conditions. Kiekolt-Glaser *et al.* (1985) found
significantly poorer DNA repair ability among depressed patients than nondepressed controls. This suggests that there may be a "direct pathway through
which distress could influence the incidence of cancer"
(Kiekolt-Glaser *et al.*, 1985, p. 311). Depressive and re-
pressive personality styles, concluded one recent review, indeed, appear to be among those characteristics
favoring cancer (Cunningham, 1985).

Summing up what is presently known about personality and disease, Friedman and Booth-Kewley
(1987) suggest:

> Personality may function like diet: Imbalances can pre-
> dispose one to all sorts of diseases. Such a conclusion is
> supported by the considerable evidence emerging from
> physiological studies. (p. 552)

Now what, may we ask, is the purported *physiological* basis for these findings? One leading theory, derived from Cannon (1929) and elaborated upon by Selye (1976), is that perceived stress is the culprit. It seems that perceived stress leads to two biochemical forms of preparedness: the urge to "fight" or to take "flight." Historically, these responses served an adaptive function. A simple cave dweller, for example, might flee a wild animal, or a hunter might kill an animal for food. Today, however, these responses tend to be maladaptive because they cannot be consummated. We cannot run away from financial troubles, career, and social demands. Likewise, we cannot kill beings or things simply because they threaten us. The result is that we are bombarded daily by "fight or flight" mechanisms that wreak havoc on our bodies (Benson, 1979).

From the standpoint of paradox, "taking flight" is related to feeling withdrawn, diminished, subdued, trapped, suffocated, or, in a word, constricted. Attendant psychiatric syndromes include depression, dependency, anxiety, and obsessive-compulsiveness (Liketsos & Liketsos, 1986). Bodily, one feels "tight," "choked off," "limp" (see Lowen, 1970). Indeed, this is what seems to happen to actual muscle and organ systems as they prepare one for retreat (Coleman, 1976). Correspondingly, flight may manifest as the sense that one cannot do the work necessary to run one's body. The body may be viewed as a sluggish, disabling machine, especially in the case of exhausted or depleted states (Becker, 1973; Selye, 1976).

"Fighting," from the standpoint of paradox, is related to feeling enlarged, engorged, explosive, tenacious, or, in short, expansive. Mood and impulse disorders are relevant here. Physically, one feels poised, pushed, stretched, or frenzied (see Lowen, 1970). The body is experienced as overly restrictive and confining (Stevick, 1979). Muscle and organ systems, likewise, strain to prepare for combat (Coleman, 1976).

Now it may be countered that although *perceived* constrictive and expansive bodily changes occur, actual physiological changes (via the sympathetic nervous system) vary only slightly between the poles (Cannon, 1929). If this is the case, one may argue, then there is no clear physiological basis for differentiating the two poles.

This prospect, however, is not a threat to the paradox principle. It only points out how far we are from finding clear experiential-physiological correlates, as pointed out earlier in this book. Moreover, it appears that in the case of at least some constrictive (flight) and expansive (fight) experiences, physiological differentiation does occur. For example, while the "flight trait" anxiety shows a similar sympathetic pattern to the "fight trait" aggression (i.e., with regard to an increase in adrenaline), other "flight traits" such as despondency and sedentary withdrawal sharply differ from "fight traits." The former (as opposed to the latter), for example, entail a *deactivation* of sympathetic reserves, and result in such "vegetative" symptoms as lowered immunity and morbid obesity (Kiekolt-Glaser *et al.*, 1985; Kobasa *et al.*, 1982; Miller, Rosellini, & Seligman, 1977).

Optimal responses, finally, are theorized to moderate fight or flight mechanisms (Kobasa, 1979). They tend to be more realistic, flexible, and tempered (see Lowen, 1970). They also tend to be more personally and socially productive, and place less strain on one's body (Kobasa *et al.*, 1982; Lowen, 1970).

To summarize, the following tentative conclusions can be drawn: chronic constriction (or "flight" responses)—hopelessness, withdrawal, repression—and expansion (or "fight" responses)—dominance, hostility, competitiveness—appear to have debilitating physical effects. Useful integrations of these dimensions, on the other hand—commitment, control, challenge, flexibility—appear to have positive bodily effects.

OPTIMAL ORGANIZATIONS

The research on organizational psychology is equally intriguing for the paradox principle. Recent studies, for example, suggest that executives who can both focus on details (constrict) and understand the broader (expansive) implications of their work are more effective. Perceptually, such ability is comparable to that of a wide-angle lens. One "teases out" the essential but places it in a cohesive (personally and socially enriching) framework as well. Garfield (1986) elaborates:

> The people getting impressive results today in successful organizations, large and small, hold overall missions in mind while they also attend to the necessary details. (p. 155)

> Analysis helps to break down a problem into manageable elements. It is not particularly helpful, however, without its partner synthesis. The value of the macroperspective is that it allows one to see innovative ways to combine the analyzed elements into a new whole. (p. 157)

Garfield (1986) goes on to illustrate this perspective with an anecdote about an auto mechanic. Dissatisfied with routine mechanical work, this man "read hungrily during lunchtime," restored "old limousines" during off-hours, and began "his own limo service, contacting corporations . . . [and] advertising in the Yellow Pages" (p. 159). The mechanic, Garfield (1986) concluded, "knew his . . . own abilities and [saw] how they fit into a continuously growing larger picture" (p. 159).

Another aspect of this "micro/macro" view is detailed by Peters and Waterman (1982), who discuss the spectrum in terms of "closed and open" systems. For the first 60 years of this century, write the theorists, management was assuredly "closed" (Peters & Waterman, 1982, p. 91). They "did not worry about the environment, competition, the marketplace, or anything else external to the organization" (Peters & Waterman, 1982, p.91). That "myopic" view, as the authors term it, did not change much until about 1960 when theorists were beginning to acknowledge the role played by forces outside the organization. This recognition thus ushered in the "open system" era (Peters & Waterman, 1982).

Still another facet of the above polarities is the split between organizational "rationality" and "social" concerns (Peters & Waterman, 1982). In formal terms, this split is captured by McGregor's theory X and theory Y respectively (Peters & Waterman, 1982). Rational theories of management, akin to closed systems, emphasize the constricting internal, logical, and quantitative aspects of corporate activity. Prevailing styles of management during the early part of this century were rational. Social theories of management, on the other hand, stressed the expansive human dimensions of corporate enterprise, and began to arise in concert with a renewed appreciation for personal and communal integrity. Whereas rational and closed systems tended to view employees as mediocre, lazy, and in need of direct control, social and open systems placed the premium on individual and group responsibility, innovation, and intelligence (Peters & Waterman, 1982). Yet what has become strikingly clear about these modalities is that neither works in isolation. Whereas the closed, rational system sacrificed human dignity, the open, socially oriented system sacrificed organizational necessities. "The overwhelming failure of the human relations movement," write Peters and Waterman (1982, p. 95), "was precisely its failure to be seen as the balance to the excesses of the rational model, a failure ordained by its own silly excesses." The authors continue:

> We are beginning to perceive, however dimly, a central theme that in our minds makes the excellent companies great. On the surface of it, Theory X and Theory Y are mutually exclusive. . . . As a leader you are authoritarian or you are democratic. In reality you are neither and both at the same time. Messrs. Watson (IBM), Kroc (McDonald's), Marriott, *et al.*, have been pathbreakers in treating people as adults . . . in providing training and development opportunities for all. . . . On the other hand, all of these gentlemen were tough as nails . . . when their core values of service to the customer . . . were violated. They combined, then, a caring side and a tough side. (Peters & Waterman, 1982, p. 96)

The importance of an integrated or well-proportioned organizational scheme has been borne out, finally, by several experimental studies. For example, Quinn (1985) found that the successful companies "accept the essential chaos of development."

> They pay close attention to their users' needs and desires, avoid detailed early technical or marketing plans,

and allow entrepreneurial teams to pursue competing alternatives within a clearly conceived framework of goals and limits. (p. 73)

House (1971), similarly, found that effective leaders blend sensitivity to the enrichment needs of group members and task-oriented initiative.

With regard to employees, Herzberg, Mausner, and Snyderman (1959) found that those who are both challenged by and appropriately responsible for a variety of tasks tend to be more satisfied than those who do not fulfill these criteria. May (1977), Weick (1984), and Yerkes and Dodson (1908), finally, found (on both subjective and objective measures) that either too much or too little arousal is vocationally dysfunctional, whereas a moderate amount is optimal.

The upshot of this data is that the best business people, like their counterparts above, are able to confront paradox. They tend to "draw back" (inspect details, define tasks, restrict funds) and "burst forth" (explore, innovate, persist) as needed. They use space and time liberally when change, participation, and sensitivity are called for, and conservatively when stability, direction, and logic are relevant. The poorer business people, by contrast, appear to be intimidated by paradox. They tend to be constrictively or expansively polarized and disabled by the prospect of bridging those poles.

OPTIMAL SOCIETIES

The best societies also appear to display paradoxical features. Although revolt and extremism are the occasional *necessary* antidote, they tend not to endure if they fail to absorb existing structures. The civil rights movement, for example, *eventually* addressed state and federal legislation. The women's movement *ultimately* penetrated business and academic establishments.

On an even larger scale, the United States itself began as a revolt, but eventually learned to address conflicting and even contradictory aims. The framers of the Constitution, for example, combined a spirit of openness and practicality. The right to "free speech and assembly" served as a check against institutional coercion. The right to vote countered oppressive legal and political practices. Mob rule was balanced by due process of law. Congress served as a check against the President. The Supreme Court served as a check against the Congress. The people served as a check against the Supreme Court (e.g., by electing legislators who can amend the Constitution). And all three served as checks against each other (Hamilton, Madison, & Jay, 1982).

The democratic system of checks and balances, writes Schlesinger (1986),

> assumes neither total perfectibility nor total depravity. It sees humans simultaneously as tainted by original sin and as capable of redemption. The democratic way by no means guarantees the triumph of virtue. . . . Still, the exercise of dissent and opposition tempers the delusions of power. (p. 434)

He concludes: "Democracy rests solidly on the mixed view of human nature, on people as they are in all their frailty and glory" (Schlesinger, 1986, pp. 434–435).

The struggle between public and private interest is another facet of the above spectrum. Because many societies rebuff dissent, they become polarized at the communal or private levels. However, democratic societies are less likely to become polarized because at least some dissent is tolerated (Schlesinger, 1986). For example, the more American society swings toward private interest, the more people begin to acknowledge public priorities. Conversely, the more people shift toward the state, the more they start to see the value of private institutions (Schlesinger, 1986). The upshot of this scenario is that American life is to a great extent cyclical. When the outgroup gets tired of the ingroup, the outgroup can to some extent be integrated periodically. Although this is not the optimal melding of contrasting views, it is among the best frameworks nations have.

Certain communes or intentional societies, on the other hand, appear to place an even higher value on confronting and integrating differences. Campbell (1983, p. 180) writes that intentional groups prize "synergistic," "both/and," and "paradoxical" thinking over "analytic," "either/or," and "sequential" thinking.

Such thinking, according to Campbell (1983), is associated with improved physical and psychological health, social and environmental relationships. We have already discussed several effects "paradoxical" or integrative thinking has on the mind—for example, reduced tension and conflict, increased capacity for exploration, fewer dysfunctional symptoms, and increased capacity for productivity and meaningfulness in life. We have also looked at the effects of such perception on the body—fewer organic symptoms, improved neuroendocrine and cardiovascular functioning. But what about paradoxical thinking and interpersonal relationships? What are the effects here?

Campbell (1983) points to several: First, she found that such thinking promotes a more realistic understanding of others. For example, intentional community members, Campbell (1983) reports, display less than average dichotomous thinking. They show less of an "us/them," "she's perfect or evil" mentality. Moreover, members seemed to be able to perceive one another less categorically and more in terms of particular acts or situations. As a result, it appeared that members learned more from and communicated better with one another (Campbell, 1983).

Second, because members were less afraid of one another, there appeared to be greater sharing and openness. For example, when resources were scarce, ways were found to cooperate over those resources rather than to selfishly hoard them (Campbell, 1983).

Problem solving among communitarians also fits a more integrated pattern. Instead of breaking problems up into clear-cut cause-effect relations, such as "the husband withdraws because the wife nags," adaptive members were more cognizant of the gestalt. Thus, it may be, referring to the above example, that not only does the husband withdraw because the wife nags, but that the wife nags because the husband withdraws (Campbell, 1983, p. 180). Campbell (1983, p. 180) calls this "mutually interactive" cause and effect, and concludes that, as one member put it: "To know the whole truth on any matter, it is necessary to hear and respect the many different vantage points from which the event may be viewed" (p. 134).

This assertion echoes Campbell's (1980, 1983) third stage of romantic love—"stability." The first two stages are "romance" and "power struggle," which center almost exclusively on opposition. However, stability, for Campbell (1980, 1983, pp. 128–29), supersedes the previous two stages, in that the couple now begins to recognize their commonalities as well as conflicts. For example, the wife may now begin to see that the husband's withdrawal is a legitimate need for privacy, and that she has similar feelings at times. Likewise, the husband may begin to realize that his wife's nagging actually represents a plea for togetherness, which he also values. These realizations can help the couple sort out and accept what is important to them. Or, as Campbell (1983) puts it, they

> get an idea that a . . . relationship can be a source of learning. They also find that when they are able to communicate about their differences, they eventually come to see these differences from a new and expanded perspective—a perspective which includes both viewpoints. (p. 129)

This latter recognition also paves the way for Campbell's (1983) last two stages, "commitment" and "co-creation." When couples commit to one another, they decide that their relationship is worth pursuing in all its vicissitudes. They begin to see that their common bond to love, to grow, and to learn from each other outweighs the wrenching differences that threaten to split them in two. They begin to value the time it takes to work out differences and the endurance required to tolerate uncertain times (Campbell, 1980, 1983).

In the co-creation stage, couples take what they have learned about each other and apply it to their surroundings, the world. That is, they begin conceiving of the *world* as a lover, and attempt to reconcile "otherness" where it is relevant to them. Thus, for example, couples who have moved on to this stage show a greater ability to resolve personal projects, as well as those pertaining to their communities, or society at large (Campbell, 1980, 1983; see also Maslow, 1968).

The key theme here is the movement toward *coexistence*. The more one is able to tolerate and learn from differences, without having to compromise the core of one's own uniqueness, the more adaptive one (and others) will be. Campbell (1983) concludes that

> Western society seems to be evolving toward a new, more spacious view of relationships—one which allows and encourages a wider diversity of couple and family lifestyles. At the same time, we seem to be evolving away from such scarcity-based assumptions as "relationships should make each person feel safe and secure" or "you can only love one person intimately at a time." A more spacious view of relationships was being pioneered in the Earth Community groups I visited. Spaciousness was revealed in an increased emphasis on the importance of friendship; a declining of sexual possessiveness; an increased respect for individual differences and uniqueness; and in a tendency to include in one's sense of family, people (and relatives) other than one's blood relatives. (p. 126)

Although Campbell can sound overly idealistic at points, and perhaps a bit hyperexpansive in terms of love relationships, her message is notable. It strikes at the heart of the paradoxic agenda: to confront "death" (otherness, infinitude), to transform it, and to fashion it into something proportionate, adaptive, or innovative.

At the same time, Campbell's message has a proud and enduring philosophical heritage. Writers such as Eric Fromm, Martin Buber, Maurice Merleau-Ponty, Simone de Beauvoir and a host of others have been laying its foundation for years (see Sadler's, 1969, wonderfully comprehensive review and Bellah *et al.*, 1985). Witness Buber (1967), for example, on Jewish social philosophy:

This . . . is . . . Judaism's fundamental significance for mankind: that, conscious as is no other community of the primal dualism, knowing and typifying division more than any other community, it proclaims a world in which dualism will be abolished, a world of God which needs to be realized in both the life of individual man and the life of the community: the world of unity. (p. 33)

Or Fromm (1956) on the "paradoxical character" of love:

We are all One—yet every one of us is a unique, unduplicable entity. In our relationships to others the same paradox is repeated. . . . Love of one person implies love of man as such. (pp. 47, 50)

From this it [also] follows that my own self must be as much an object of my love as another person. *The affirmation of one's own life, happiness, growth, freedom is rooted in one's capacity to love*, i.e., in care, respect, responsibility, and knowledge. (p. 50)

Robert Solomon (1981) affirms this: "The paradox of love," he states, "is . . . that it presupposes a strong sense of individual autonomy and independence, and then seeks to cancel this by creating a shared identity" (pp. 25–26; see also McDevitt & Mahler, 1980).

The essential point here is that interpersonal or group action demands the critical exercise of *choice*. Rather than shirking this problem off or bolting in panic, the person or people must attempt to work with it. They must *reflect upon* the constrictive or expansive demands of a situation, and ferret out the *optimal* courses of action. The civil rights movement, as we have shown, engaged this process. Whereas neither violence nor passivity could achieve their intended aims (e.g., to elevate the status of American blacks), black leadership chose a route between the two. Nonviolent protest, they found, both avoided the negative consequences and (partially) met the aims of the other two courses of action. This is precisely the kind of paradoxic, integrationist tack that must endure.

Campbell (1983) concurs:

> Back and forth we have swung, between overcontrol and overflexibility—Hawks and Doves, Hard-hats and Hippies, and so forth.
> But the time has come for a synthesis of these apparent dualities. Our culture seems to be moving toward a new identity, somewhere between these extremes. (pp. 178–179)

Are the hints of democracy ("glasnost") in the Soviet Union, private ownership in China, and nationalized health care in the United States the forerunners to this "new identity"? We can only hope they are.

OPTIMAL DEVELOPMENT

If tolerance for and adaptive redirection of paradox mark the best adult relationships, then similar elements should be operational for children. Indeed, researchers are beginning to find that extreme (constrictive or expansive) parenting styles have extreme effects on children. Similarly, more proportional styles have more proportional effects.

Although the childhoods of optimal adults, especially the most indisputably gifted, are far from smooth, or neatly "packaged," they do reveal several common threads: The parents of these children, for example, tend to combine *both* supportive warmth and relevant firmness (Baumrind, 1971; Janos & Robinson, 1985;

Thomas & Chess, 1977). They tend neither to over- or understimulate their children, but provide the amount appropriate to the child's age and ability (Elkind, 1987; Emde, 1985; Meyerhoff & White, 1986; Trotter, 1987). When tragedy strikes—which appears to be relatively often in gifted families, due in part perhaps to their nonconforming nature (Farson, 1974; McGoldrick & Gerson, 1985)—at least one of the parents (or caretakers) tends to be resilient (Goertzels & Goertzels, 1962). That parent's mastery, in turn, is likely to be a source of inspiration to the gifted child, and serves to help him or her cope (Bergin & Lambert, 1978; Goertzels & Goertzels, 1962; McGoldrick & Gerson, 1985).

Indeed, there is an indication, as we discussed in an earlier section, that tragedy and its subsequent management are pivotal for the gifted child. If he never learns to face or handle it properly, he may become a psychological cripple; or equally unfortunate, a "dullard" who never "lives up to his potential" (see Farson, 1974). If he never learns to face and integrate the contradictions in his life, as the paradox principle intimates, he will continue to treat constriction and expansion as burdens to be *endured* rather than challenges to be *engaged*.

Many of those who later express their talents, on the other hand, avert this fate. Specifically, such people may *begin* as the victims of acute, chronic, or implicit traumas—they may *start out* dysfunctionally focused, deferent, incorporating, or assertive, as a result. However, in contrast to the former group, someone (or something) helps them to "hone" and constructively redirect those dispositions. Someone, in other words, helps them to productively *harness* and *apply* their constrictive or expansive excesses.

Specific studies bear out the value of integrative childhood experiences. Bergin and Lambert (1978), for example, discuss a youth who emerged from an extremely dysfunctional background. Every member of his family, they report, except for the youth himself, was hospitalized for a mental illness. And yet the boy grew up to *excel* at school, sports, and a government position. After examining this boy's background, the investigators found that two people—both from a neighborhood family—appeared to be instrumental in his success. One was an older boy whom he looked up to as a role model. The other was the older boy's mother who appeared to offer just the kind of integrative relationship necessary for the youth. The researchers conclude that the youth's relationship to her was "emotionally" nurturant, but "not symbiotic, and seemed to foster his independence and self-development" (Bergin & Lambert, 1978, p. 150).

Drevdahl (1964) came to a similar conclusion about a sample of eminent psychologists he studied. He found that his subjects appeared

> to have been given early independence combined with responsibility—much more so than either the noncreative productive or noncreative nonproductive group— and to have received somewhat more family, rather than nonfamily, pressure for achievement, but always within a less emotive and frantic atmosphere than the other groups. (p. 177)

In a large-scale study of parents and their nursery school-age children, Baumrind (1971) found that the best parents were neither overly strict nor overly accepting but "authoritative." Authoritative parents, according to her study, fostered responsible and independent children, whereas authoritarian and permissive parents produced socially irresponsible, overly dependent, rebellious, and incompetent children.

After some 25 years of educational research, Meyeroff and White (1986) conclude:

> [The best] parents were not afraid to set realistic but firm boundaries on behavior before their children's first birthday. During the first months of life, these parents lavished love and attention on their children and responded almost unconditionally to every demand. However, starting at about 8 months, and especially during the normal period of "negativism" between 15 and 24 months of age, when many children's demands were simply tests of what they could get away with, these parents reacted by letting the children know in no uncertain terms that other people had rights too. (p. 45)

These findings parallel those of Kagan, Thomas and Chess, and others who have also conducted extensive research with children and their families. Kagan stated summarily, "parents need to push their children—gently and not too much—into doing the things they fear" (Quoted in Asher, 1987, p. 64).

Based on a large-scale observational study of infants, Stechler and Kaplan (1980) suggest that optimal parents

> (1) recognize [their] child's intention; (2) respond to it in a fairly consistent way; (3) communicate back to the child sufficiently clear, consistent signals so that the child knows what their reaction is; (4) permit the sequence to go far enough so the child (a) has a sense of intention, (b) carries the act to fruition, and (c) receives some kind of messsage about the consequences of her action. (p. 102)

The authors present an exemplary case illustration of such integrated parenting:

> Thus, we note that Nancy's parents combined a clearly expressed definiteness about limits and prohibitions with a reasonable degree of flexibility. In general, they displayed a very nice balance in responding to Nancy, permitting her wide latitude and freedom within a framework of clearly defined, consistent, yet not always inexorable limits. Nancy adapted to this surround, accepted restraints, and gradually developed the capacity to impose limits on herself. (p. 100)

Nancy's ability to "impose limits on herself" was illustrated by a cube-throwing incident. During a cube design task, Nancy repeatedly and haphazardly scattered them onto the floor. Her mother began to grow impatient with this behavior. When Nancy attempted to throw the cubes onto the floor again her mother aborted the attempt. Nancy then gestured as if to do the same thing, but this time slowly released a cube at the table's edge. This was considered acceptable by the mother and seen as a "creative transformation of [a] conflict between [a] wish and [a] prohibition" by the observers (Stechler & Halton, 1987, p. 825).

Related to the above, optimal parents communicate more effectively with their children. Children are able to "hear" parental messages that are guised in firm yet receptive terms, rather than dogmatic or faint-hearted terms. As Kagan points out, even children who are temperamentally polarized, such as the excessively shy, can become considerably more adaptive with parental help (reported in Asher, 1987). His studies show convincingly that the best parents walk a fine, artistically managed line with their children. They are able to invite them into threatening psychological situations (such as social occasions for the shy), yet sense how to curb children from such moments, so as to avoid worsening their dispositions (reported in Asher, 1987). It is in this kind of interplay that children learn to reconcile both original and acquired behaviors for fuller, more productive lives (see also Kohut, 1977, on "transmuting internalizations").

Elkind (1987) provides a spirited recap of these findings:

> Our trouble is that we always seem to go to extremes. Parents are either too permissive or too pushy. Healthy child rearing demands a middle ground. Certainly we need to make demands on our children. But they have to be tailored to the child's interests and abilities. We put our children at risk for short-term stress disorders and long-term personality problems when we ignore their individuality and impose our own priorities "for their own good." (p. 61)

Was it not Elkind's mentor, Piaget (1971), who stressed "equilibrium" in the child's relations with his or her environment? "All cognitive construction (a creative process itself)," he wrote, "depends on a series of dynamic interactions in which the factors at play do not consist only of positive 'forces' but also of resistances to be overcome" (Quoted in Gruber, 1984, pp. viii, ix).

What can we now say empirically about optimal development? First, there is mounting evidence of an optimal constrictive/expansive parenting style. Parents who are overly confining or overly tolerant foster similar or proportionately reverse behavior in their offspring. Parents or caretakers, on the other hand, who address their children's constrictive and expansive capacities at given periods help their children grow in a centered, "freer" manner.

CONCLUSION ON THE EMPIRICAL STATUS OF OPTIMAL CONFRONTATIONS

In summary, I proposed that the confrontation with and redirection of constrictive/expansive potentialities can, in the "right" degree, have an optimal and enriching outcome. This outcome was further proposed to encompass large areas of personal and social life.

Accordingly, there appears to be a growing body of evidence to support this view. These data derive from the domains of personological, physiological, organizational, social, and developmental psychology. It would seem worthwhile to pursue these lines of research. An effort to be more specific about constrictive and expansive effects on mind and body will clarify the range within which people can embrace paradox, and hence life.

Next, we will examine what some perceive as the supreme expression of human awareness—religious or "transpersonal" confrontations with paradox.

OPTIMAL WORSHIP: CONFRONTING THE PARADOXES OF RELIGION

The question for human life is: . . . What is the "best" illusion under which to live? Or what is the most legitimate foolishness? If you are going to talk about life-enhancing illusion, then you can truly try to answer the question of which is "best" in terms that are directly meaningful to man, related to his basic conditions and needs. I think the whole question would be answered in terms of how much freedom, dignity, and hope a given illusion provides.
—Ernest Becker

For years now, existential psychology has attempted to steer clear of what it perceives as two pitfalls in the modern understanding of health: psychoanalytic pessimism and transpersonal optimism. The former view, as we have seen, reduces health to the satisfaction of instinctual drives, social adjustment, and a regressive (as opposed to proactive) imagination. The latter view grew out of a patent dissatisfaction with this restricted framework, and a zealous bid to expand it. Spearheaded by Jung, the transpersonal psychology movement was (and is) an attempt to recover the cosmic "wholeness" (or unitive experience) that Freud so tersely dismissed.[3] More recently, theorists such as Ken Wilber (1981) have taken Jung's beliefs a step further. They insist that some people can attain (and actually have attained) *total* cosmic unity.[4]

The problem with the latter view, however, is that it is highly improbable, irrelevant (for the most part) to people's concerns, and rather unappealing as formulated. While I agree that the psychological dimension is ultimately the realm of the religious, I strongly disagree with the Wilberian *inferences* regarding the latter. In an effort to deify consciousness, Wilberians have forfeited that which is realistic, practical, and inspiring to people. They have sacrificed our limited yet challenging "core."

While I have elaborated on this critique elsewhere (Schneider, 1987, 1989), I presently wish to turn tables and set forth an existential, or more precisely, paradox-based alternative to the aforementioned.[5]

---

[3]Freud (1966, p. 72) viewed the unitive experience or "oceanic feeling," as he put it, as infantile or psychotically regressed.

[4]While Jung (1963, p. 354) idealized the unitive experience, he stopped short of believing it could actually be attained.

[5]I do not wish to imply that existential theology is unique with regard to embracing paradox. As I will show, traditional religions

The foundation for this "paradoxic" view is the existential and pragmatic works of Becker (1973), Buber (1965), James (1963), May (1981), Rorty (1979), and Tillich (1952, 1967).

The first premise of this view is that there is nothing certain about human being.

The second premise is that the basis of religious (as well as moral, ethical, and epistemological) claims is practicality and trust. The degree of practicality and trust, moreover, must be of such a magnitude that one feels powerless in their absence.

Traditional religions, for example, fit this proposal eminently. First, they largely *work*, that is, they provide a coherent picture of the world and relieve people's suffering. Second, they are relied upon (*trusted*) to help people, even if they don't immediately deliver. Third, they are perceived as *central* to people's sense of security.

It should be evident from this discussion that the concept of traditional religion must be broadened to include secular ways of living (Tillich, 1967). For example, Marxism, capitalism, psychoanalysis, and vocational, recreational, and interpersonal devotions of all sorts can also be based on the sort of practicality and trust mentioned above, and therefore be termed religious.[6]

---

also affirm contradictions and can therefore be termed "paradoxical." However, the existential view, in my opinion, stands *readiest* to affirm paradox, and that is why I adopt it. I am grateful to Rollo May for helping me to clarify this point.

[6]Interestingly, the Latin root of "religion" is "religare," which means, literally, to "bind back"—the very process required to be practical and trust someone or something (*Webster's New World Dictionary*, 1968, p. 1228).

The third premise is that because practicality and trust form the apex of what can be consciously experienced, religions or beliefs which try to exceed these conditions arrive at one of two paths. The first path is what the Greeks termed "hubris" and what Rollo May (1981) termed "mistaking freedom for destiny." This is the direction of wishful thinking, presumption, and deceit. Those who believe human beings have achieved ultimate or infinite consciousnesss, for example, are representatives of this path.

The second path is the "truth" of the human condition without structure, vision, or guidance. This is the path of insanity (Becker, 1973, p. 147).

Becker (1973) elaborates:

> No organismic life can be straightforwardly self-expansive in all directions; each one must draw back into himself in some areas, pay some penalty of a severe kind for his natural fears and limitations. It is all right to say, with Adler, that mental illness is due to "problems in living,"—but we must remember that life itself is the insurmountable problem. (p. 270)

Even atheists and agnostics are not exempt from Becker's declaration. For example, the reason that Freud "could so easily confess his agnosticism," insisted Rank (1941, p. 272), was because "he had created his own private religion." "Something is holy to everyone," Tillich (1967) expounds, "even to those who deny the holy" (p. 130).

So the question for a paradoxic understanding of religion is not which one is "right," or whether people can live without it, but which one is most helpful (personally, socially, potentially, or the like), and most worthy of commitment.

The existential, and in turn, paradoxic position regarding this question is a complex one. This is so because, first, there are a variety of existential theological positions. Second, these positions are often shrouded in esoteric or abstract terms. However, inasmuch as Becker (1973) has given us one of the most lucid and persuasive summaries of these positions, his work will form the basis for my exposition here.

The most pragmatic and trustworthy religion, according to Becker (1973), is Kierkegaard's "knight of faith" concept (without its strict appeal to Christianity), which is also a variant of Tillich's "courage to be," Buber's "I-thou," and James' religious "pragmatism."

Stated baldly, this position asserts that people strive for the most fulfilled, socially productive relationships of which they are capable, then "surrender to" the forces which supersede these parameters. Becker (1973) elaborates:

> The religious geniuses of history have argued that to be really submissive means to be submissive to the highest power, the true infinity, the absolute—and not to any human substitutes, lovers, leaders, nation-states. (p. 251)

Such submissiveness, however, is not an ethereal involvement, continues Becker (1973), but a forceful "confrontation of potential meaninglessness" (p. 280). It requires the "boldest creative myths, not only to urge [people] on, but also to see the reality of their condition. We have to be as hard-headed as possible about reality and possibility" (p. 280).

Loving thy neighbor as thyself, for example, is one of those great "bold myths" that Becker alludes to. This theme manifested throughout the ages in terms of kindness and caring, tolerance for diversity, egalitarianism, and staunch antiauthoritarianism. However, the admonishment informs little (even in its ideal form) about basic human predicaments. It does not tell us, for instance, about when to separate from troubled relationships. It does not explain how to eliminate catastrophies, disasters, and maladies of all sorts. It sheds little light on the problem of cruelty.[7] It skirts the problem of individualism. Finally, it does not relieve us of the ultimate problem, *Uncertainty*.

This is why Gandhi, King, Jesus, and other prophets *struggled* so. None of them—it seems—could solve the final puzzles of living and each was confined to a framework. For Gandhi, that framework was nonviolent resistance, sovereignty for the individual and state, and "Moshka" or surrender to the divine (Erik-

---

[7] There is little evidence that love alone (as it is traditionally conceived) can quell brutality—courage, common sense, and even force may be needed as well (Berman, 1989). Philosopher Phillip Hallie (cited in Moyers, 1988) illustrated this point in his discussion of a Nazi-occupied French village at the outbreak of World War II. Le Chambon, as it is called, epitomized the biblical ideal, according to Hallie. Not only was the community extraordinarily forebearing toward its citizens and those it harbored, but also toward those who victimized it. The town was especially interested, as Hallie intimated, in *saving* Nazis (cited in Moyers, 1988, p. 7). They wanted to convert them through love. The upshot of this scenario, however, was that the opposite occurred. Soon after 1940, Nazi officials, and even Hitler himself, sent letters of praise to the town. "Thank you very much," these letters stated, "you've been very helpful to us by not fighting, and by discouraging people from fighting" (cited in Moyers, 1988, p. 7).

"A thousand Le Chambons," Hallie concluded, "would not have stopped Hitler" (cited in Moyers, 1988, p. 7). "It took decent murderers like me to do it" (cited in Moyers, 1988, p. 7).

son, 1975). For King and Jesus it was a similar stance, coupled with a belief in heavenly redemption. That these men toiled magnanimously and improved humanity's lot there is little debate. But—and this is Becker's key point—they each gave up at their earthly limit and entrusted God or powers beyond them to take control.

Going as far as one can go and giving up at the very apex of one's powers is also the prime characteristic of Eastern mysticism. Buddha, for example, believed in eradicating humanity's desires (and therefore tormenting expectations). He did this not to solve the problem of immortality but to *reduce* suffering. "I do not know," Buddha was quoted as having responded to a question about whether the cosmos is eternal, "and it is of no concern to me because whatever the answer is it does not contribute to the one problem which is of concern; how to reduce human suffering" (quoted in Fromm, 1950, p. 105).

Bharati (1976), noted writer and mystic, explains that the Buddha refused to confer divine status to his perspective because he knew "that nothing ontological followed from his experience" (p. 85).

Thus, even Buddha had his "God," outside of which he was lost, and, in all likelihood, uninterested.

Taoist philosophy is another example of optimal theorizing but eventual capitulation. In this case, it is nature that is appealed to as the elixir for most ills. It is the balance of the ecosystem, the logic of the seasons, the gracefulness of animal instincts, and the nurturance of the soil that are to be emulated (see Lao Tzu, 1955; Watts, 1975). And yet living "naturally" fails to address our need to query, alter, and reshape the future. It emphasizes reaction, not proaction, and can therefore only

be considered a partial support. Again, we are not en-
lightened about our awesome predicament.

"Even with numerous groups of liberated people,
at their best," Becker (1973) concludes,

> we can't imagine that the world will be any pleasanter
> or less tragic a place. It may even be worse in still un-
> known ways. As Tillich warned us, New Being, under
> the conditions and limitations of existence, will only
> bring . . . new and sharper paradoxes, new tensions,
> and more painful disharmonies. (p. 281)

"Reality is remorseless," Becker (1973) follows up, "because gods do not walk upon the earth, and if men
could become noble repositories of great gulfs of nonbeing, they would have even less peace than we oblivious
and driven madmen have today" (p. 281).

It is for these reasons that I propose a modified
view of religious practice—"optimal" or "paradoxic" religion. This position evaluates religion critically. How
(constrictively and expansively) liberating is it? How
much does it affirm *both* our need to yield and assert,
withdraw and affiliate, concretize and transcend? How
practical and trustworthy is it? While the biblical and
mystical traditions—as we have seen—offer *some* encouraging answers to these questions, they are by no
means definitive. Sociologists, psychoanalysts, humanists, "liberation theologians," and Darwinians also offer
some encouraging answers, and should be heeded as
well. An optimal religion prepares to draw from each.

It also follows from the optimal perspective that
what Wilber and others view as "ultimate" (e.g., the
unitive experience) is really only a stage—albeit an am-
bitious one—on life's way. For it is so-called holistic and
transpersonal psychology that must be subsumed un-

der the existential umbrella, and not the reverse (see the illustration on p. 143; also see Tillich, 1952). This is because "true" (or "trans") mysticism has no boundary, sense of purpose, or guiding vision. The true mystic, as we have seen, is lost and fully ostracized. He has no communal appeal, no ability to "bind-back" and digest the experiences undergone. His world is one of *unabating* reflection, symbolism, and ritualism, and simply cannot be systematized. Mark Vonnegut (1975), acknowledged veteran of true mysticism, puts it this way:

> Most descriptions of mystical states, while they include feelings of timelessness, actually cover very little clock time. For the schizophrenic it's a twenty-four-hour day, seven days a week. Realizing the transient nature of material things helps for a while, but it's got its limits. (p. 269)

In conclusion, religious syntheses are vast and varied, often extending beyond the individual, culture, and even history of ideas, but they do not appear to span infinity. There are two basic reasons why I have come to this conclusion: (1) Coherent, organized people who report infinite wisdom appear to live infinitely short of that wisdom (see Muzika, 1988; Schneider, 1987). (2) Incoherent, disorganized people who report infinite wisdom appear closer to living that wisdom, but vastly incapable of mastering it (Schneider, 1987).

Given these conditions, an optimal form of worship could be a refreshing change for humanity. While embracing a *sense* of the "divine" (e.g., God, Spirit), it would avoid dogmatic *presumptions* regarding the latter. While celebrating the *many* "truths," it would resist attempts to forsake *responsibility* for those "truths."

Chapter Six

TOWARD A PARADOX-BASED THERAPY AND A THERAPEUTIC RAPPROCHEMENT

If there is tragic limitation in life there is also possibility. What we call maturity is the ability to see the two in some kind of balance in which we can fit creatively.

—Ernest Becker

Recently, there has been a growing interest in psychotherapeutic unification or "rapprochement." (Goldfried, 1982; Norcross, 1986). There are several sound reasons for this. For one, eclectic therapists, in light of such a consensus, could apply their interventions with greater specificity. Second, orthodox practitioners could be prodded to broaden their skills where relevant (Norcross, 1986).

Moreover, therapeutic rapprochement should have a significant diagnostic value. A clearer consensus could be forged among practitioners as to which kinds of problems should be accorded which kinds of treatment modalities (Strupp, 1978). For example, clients with strictly symptomatic concerns might be offered commensurate behavioral interventions; those with explicitly Oedipal issues could be directed to psychoanalytic practitioners; and those with lifestyle or philosophical concerns could be provided some form of existential support.

The basis for these interventions would depend on three key elements: (1) the client's desire and capacity for change; (2) the therapist's ability to deliver services relevant to that desire and capacity; and (3) the degree of empirical support (both quantitative and qualitative, as relevant) to justify the use of select procedures (Norcross, 1986).

It is in this light, then, that the development of what I term "paradox-analysis" may be useful.[1] Paradox-analysis (as with other existential therapies) is based on one overarching principle: engage what is *relevant*—to this client, at this particular moment, in this particular setting (see Bugental, 1978; Yalom, 1980).

The thrust of a paradox-analysis, in accordance with the paradox principle, is to help people regain constrictive or expansive possibilities. The therapeutic task, then, for a hyperconstrictive individual would be to optimize his or her expansive possibilities. The reverse would be true for a hyperexpansive person. Binswanger (1975) succinctly lays the groundwork for this thesis:

> What we call psychotherapy is basically no more than an attempt to bring the patient to the point where he can "see" the manner in which the totality of human exis-

[1]Although "paradoxical intention" and dialectical therapies are similar to and can be used as a part of the paradox-analytic procedure, they cannot be fully equated with it. The former strategies, by contrast, are based on somewhat different sets of assumptions and theoretical traditions (see Frankl, 1969; Riegel, 1976).

tence or "being in the world" is structured and to see at which of its junctures he has overreached himself. (p. 348)

The question, of course, is how to facilitate such a plan. How does a therapist help an entrenched, polarized individual become adaptive and integrated? The following is a rough sketch, based on existential principles and my own clinical work, as to how paradox-analysis can proceed.

First, a paradox-analyst must sensitively attend to both clients' stated and implicit therapeutic aims (Bugental, 1981). The analyst must not only teach but also *invite* therapeutic change (Jourard, 1968). For example, many phobics fear more than specific objects but the entire "meaning-context" which underlies those objects, such as associations to helplessness, humiliation, and death (May, 1977; Wolfe, 1988). A paradox-analyst, therefore, might help a (constrictive) phobic with exposure treatments (Marks, 1978), but he would provide more figurative opportunities for that client to expand as well, e.g., through caring, empathy, humor, body "language," exploration of symbolic life, and so on. Such offerings evoke the phobic at the meaning-level of his dread and pave the way, if appropriate, for more fundamental (that is, experiential) changes.[2] Similarly, sociopathic expansiveness can be stemmed by overt

[2]I share the existential therapeutic bias that experiential, internal, or centric-level change is necessary for *fundamental* client-change. Interestingly, a small but growing body of research is beginning to confirm this view (see Aron & Aron, 1987; Green, Wilson, & Lovato, 1986; Maher & Nadler, 1986; Wolfe, 1988). While extrinsic or symptomatic therapies may be helpful to those with limited situation-specific aims, "intrinsic" therapies appear to be necessary for value and lifestyle concerns.

limit-setting techniques (e.g., aversive conditioning), coupled with the aforementioned attitudes (see Bugental, 1976; Kazdin, 1978).

To embellish further, every behavior that associates with the "core" (constrictive or expansive) fears is analyzable from this perspective—thoughts, feelings, gestures, reveries, intentions. The paradox-analyst does not feel constrained by either technique or "target" behaviors, only by those strategies and aims which emerge as appropriate. Anxiety, as a rule, is the analyst's best guide. The more anxious the client becomes, the less he can *relinquish* his extremism, the closer he is to his core fears, and the clearer the analyst becomes about what "invitation" is necessitated (see Bugental, 1978).

To state this approach more succinctly: The paradox-analyst attempts to (1) survey the associational network of clients' extremism—the patterns and situations in which clients perceive in a "hyper" manner; and (2) engage the constrictive or expansive alternatives available to rearrange (or integrate) that network.

This procedure is a very delicate one, as can be surmised. Many clients are polarized at different levels of awareness at different points in time (see Frank, 1973; Truax, Carkhuff, & Kodman, 1965). Much of the work, then, consists in careful prioritizing of clients' concerns and the capacity to help them work through each one accordingly.

For example, I had a client who, on the surface, had the classic constrictive/depressive profile. He was plagued by guilt, self-denigration, and social alienation. However, as we proceeded, it became clear that interventions aimed at *expanding* this client's sense of self were only partially effective. At a deeper level, he emerged as narcissistic and rageful. *Constriction* was his dreaded enemy. He felt guilty, self-denigrating, and reserved, therefore, not because of past repression, but because of past *overgratification*. He was familiar with doing things he wanted to do when he wanted to do them, and as soon as this agenda could not be met, he felt "guilty" and dejected as a result. Hence, this client's confrontation with *constrictive* experiences— deprivation, uncertainty, and delay of gratification— proved to be the ultimately effective strategy.

Overall, then, it is of vital importance that the analyst empathically prioritize clients' concerns. She must sense when to press and when to yield, when to instruct and when to disclose. She must run a careful course between *minimizing* clients' exacerbation potential (i.e., potential for retrauma) and *maximizing* their awareness potential (i.e., potential for constrictive or expansive encounter). She must match (to the degree appropriate) open body stances with rigid ones; contained replies with explosive ones; solicitous responses with reticent ones; and so on. This is the art.

These therapeutic "matches" struck me as particularly significant during my doctoral work. In a phenomenological analysis of "clients' perceptions of the positive and negative characteristics of their counselors" (Schneider, 1984), I found that the "best" counselors were considered "balanced." They were adept, not so much at specialized techniques or glowing expressions, but at the timing and modulation of these offerings. They sensed when and to what extent to "push" clients. For example, one interviewee and former client stated:

[My therapist left] me enough room to struggle for
awhile. She gave me a chance to experience what I was
experiencing before she explained it. . . . She'd never
push but she wouldn't leave me out there too long.
(Schneider, 1984, p. 109)

Another interviewee, "Mike," said about his counselor:

There was a skill in . . . knowing when to hang out . . . ,
when to do something . . . , when to ask a question, or
make a suggestion. And with techniques, knowing
when to use them and when not to. (Schneider, 1984, p.
107)

Still another interviewee, "Ellen," reported:

He'd say what he felt, but tactfully. Sometimes, if it
wasn't the appropriate time he'd react but wouldn't say
something overtly. (Schneider, 1984, p. 107)

Finally, another interviewee, "Sam," addressed the
specific result of his counselor's timing:

Maybe he had a sense of what's good for people. Push-
ing me wouldn't have given me the sense of my power,
it would have come from the outside. . . . I went into
the seminary when I was 13. In a sense they took control
of my life. . . . [And] it's like looking at the power outside instead of within. (Schneider, 1984, p. 109)

On the negative side, interviewees felt that counselors were either *too* personally involved (i.e., needy,
demanding, vulnerable) or not involved enough. They
also found counselors to be either *too* formal and rigid or
overly informal and unstructured. These imbalances,
reported clients, stifled their ability to confront their
fears.

"Mike," for example, described his therapist's hyperconstriction:

I felt that every time sex would come up, he would recede. . . . A lot of times it would happen physically. He would turn his chair maybe fifteen degrees from where he was facing me to where he was facing his desk. . . . I didn't know if it was his own personal problem he never dealt with or what. (Schneider, 1984, p. 118)

Mike's reaction to his therapist's action:

My response was to leave therapy. . . . At first, I felt disappointed in myself. [Like] I'm not expressing myself to [him]. . . . Then I said to [him], I don't know what's going on, I need help with this. . . . Then it became evident that I couldn't get help. . . . I feel I'm still at the same point [on my sexual problem] . . . [although] the rest of my life has come together. (Schneider, 1984, p. 127)

"Bob" also felt his counselor was not active enough:

Partly it had to do with what I expected and didn't get. . . . I felt like I needed a real kick through the door and I wasn't getting it from [my counselor]. There was some way in which I didn't feel met, some way I wanted to be confronted more. She wasn't strong enough. It was very mental. . . . The spirit of the warrior was missing. (Schneider, 1984, p. 119)

Bob's response to his counselor's apparent passivity:

It was like I could get away with too much because she was too accepting. . . . What happened was that I went through a year and a half of therapy, and I kept dealing with the same issues over and over. . . . The thing did not shift. . . . I grew wiser, but the pattern was continually there. . . . I know I would've continued therapy longer had I felt more of the charge, more of the warrior. (Schneider, 1984, p. 130)

"Alice" also perceived a lack of involvement on the part of her counselor:

> An involved person, you have a sense that they're experiencing what you're experiencing, in an empathic way. . . . I just didn't think that she ever participated in my experience except intellectually. (Schneider, 1984, p. 126)

Alice's response to this inability to expand socially:

> I didn't like it at all. It confused me because I'm aware that every client wants to feel . . . special. . . . She was extremely bland. And I don't think she was a bland person either. . . . I don't think that there was anything about the problems that I presented to her that she had simply more than a passing interest in. . . . She was responsible . . . and minimally effective in that she didn't foul me up. . . . But there was something missing. (Schneider, 1984, p. 127)

Finally, "Cindy" viewed her counselor as *overly* "charged" and involved:

> I think she had a program and I wasn't going along with it. She wanted me to do EST [Erhardt Seminar Training] and I didn't want to do EST. (Schneider, 1984, p. 135)

Cindy's response to her counselor's (expansive) demand:

> Like an idiot, I said I will [join EST]. Then I went home and felt, "I have fucking sold out!" I've never wanted this and I'm agreeing to placate this woman. . . . I was always holding back 90% of everything from her because she didn't approve. . . . I never had a deep trust. (Schneider, 1984, p. 138)

Each of these vignettes is an example, then, of integrative and imbalanced therapy styles. Counselors, like most people, appear to help others best when they themselves are integrated (Jourard, 1971). Those who have addressed and transformed their own extremes (both personally and professionally) are in better positions to address and transform others'. Let us look now at a further elaboration of therapeutic skills which can be applied paradox-analytically.

Insight training can help expansively hostile clients become more discretionary (see Freud, 1958). By pointing out a client's outmoded anger toward his father, for example, the therapist can help that client reduce his hostile disposition. By clarifying the unrealistic nature of their assumptions, cognitive therapists can help depressed clients expand their mood (Beck, 1976).

Visualization techniques can also help clients confront their fears. For example, shy and withdrawn clients might picture themselves as vigorous and assertive; careless, impulsive clients might fantasize about being disciplined and deliberate (Charlesworth & Nathan, 1982).

Meditation can promote similar changes. Concentrative meditation, which is essentially focalized attending, can help overly stimulated clients become more methodical (Brown, 1977). Mindful meditation, which refers essentially to receptive attending, can help overly reserved clients become more flexible (Brown, 1977). Awareness of body sensations and affect can also help clients optimize their potentialities. For example, the more clients are able to familiarize themselves with their fears, the more they can perceive them constructively (Bugental, 1981; Gendlin, 1978; May, 1969).

Movement skills can enhance body fluidity (Lowen, 1970). For example, contracted body postures can facilitate focalization and concentration skills (Brown,

1977); expansive body postures (e.g., aerobics) can promote vitality, elevated mood, and improved self-image
(Charlesworth & Nathan, 1982).

Role playing can lend a sense of immediacy and
actuality to clients' therapeutic efforts (Bugental, 1976).
A constrictive client can learn to expand and vice versa
by simulating and rehearsing these modalities.

To summarize, paradox-analysis aims to minimize
clients' exacerbation (retrauma) potential while maximizing their awareness (confrontation) potential. Facil-
itation of this process is both artistic and technical.

CASE ILLUSTRATIONS

Now let us examine in more detail several therapeutic cases that I have conducted which both add to
and illustrate the above applications.

Jane: A Case of Hyperexpansion

One late fall day I received a call from a local case
worker. My next client is a "child at risk," she asserted.
"She is highly temperamental, suspicious of adults, and
running her young divorced mother ragged." I soon
received a testing report confirming these concerns.

The girl whom I shall call Jane was nine years old,
and had emerged from a disruptive background. Her
father was reportedly an alcoholic and separated from
her mother when she was about four. He had not been
heard from since. According to her mother, Jane dealt
with her father's loss very poorly, becoming increasingly angry, suspicious of adults, and impulsive. Several

years later, Jane's mother became involved with an apparently congenial, warm boyfriend, who was allegedly able to become considerably close to Jane. Jane seemed to see him as the caring, loving father she never had, and often tagged along at his side. After about two years, however, all this came to an abrupt end. Jane's mother "broke up" with her boyfriend, and suddenly Jane was thrust back into a sense of being abandoned and rejected. Her behavior worsened, as she dealt with this blow doubly hard.

She began failing at school, became highly distractible, and developed an explosive temper that was especially virulent when demands were placed on her. She also became oppositional and sometimes lashed out in dangerous ways. For example, once she smashed some windows in her bedroom because she was so angry at her mother. From her mother's point of view, Jane was out of control.

By the time I saw Jane, she was so distrusting of others (especially authority) and felt so inadequate that she did everything she could to look superior. She cheated to win games or sporting events. She refused to acknowledge any weaknesses. If her efforts became thwarted at any point, she would blatantly deny reality and throw a tantrum.

Although I proceeded cautiously with Jane, she brought out all her expansive defenses at the least provocation. For example, there were numerous points while playing whiffle ball together when she would explicitly deny rules. These denials would reach exaggerated proportions. She would call pitches she threw in the dirt or over my head "strikes." When she was tagged midway to first base, she would deem herself "safe."

When such discrepancies were pointed out to her, Jane would scream with indignation. Sometimes, she would also throw things or destroy property. For a time, I tried to intensify my support for her during these confrontations. I might say things like, "This may be hard for you to accept or may not be what you're used to, but I am honestly *not* trying to hurt you when I point out these rules. I want to show you that sometimes they make you safer or make the game more enjoyable." Despite these efforts, however, Jane still could not *hear* me. I still came across as one who meant to crush her expansive (i.e., affiliative, assertive, energetic) needs.

After some agonizing over these and similar incidents, including, to no avail, the placement of consequences on Jane's actions, such as the elimination of a relevant activity, my supervisor helped me formulate a plan. This plan, as I reflect on it, was integral to Jane's subsequent improvement.

In paradox-analytic terms, the plan was to help Jane understand and integrate appropriate constriction. Given that past interventions had repeatedly failed, it was clear that this new strategy would have to be artfully engaged. It was decided, accordingly, that I would permit (to the degree possible) Jane's hyperexpansive resistances. In so doing, it was hoped, Jane would begin to see their maladaptiveness.

Thus, Jane and I engaged in the same activities described above, except that I altered my responses. Instead of attempting to explain to her the difficulties of her responses, or to impose reinforcing consequences, I fully accepted her behavior. For example, when she would protest the loss of a point, or the operation of a rule, I would tell her something like, "That's fine, Jane, you can change the rule any time you like."

Quite rapidly, probably within three weeks of this approach, Jane's oppositionality decreased considerably. Although there were still points at which she became verbally explosive, she began to smile more and started to see the humor in her demands. She also became increasingly *bored* by her triumphs. After about three months (with my gradual influence), Jane began to acknowledge the advantages of appropriate structure. She began to see that rules and less explosive behavior not only may promote safety but also may enhance her own and others' interest in given activities. She also began to realize, I believe, that the imposition of structure does not necessarily imply that she was being rejected or abandoned.

Jane's behavior improved remarkably according to school reports. She raised her grades significantly and she no longer appeared to be a management problem in class. Although her mother reported only slight behavioral improvement at home, she did note a significant overall improvement outside the home.

In concluding this vignette, let me note that therapeutic acceptance of clients' resistance is more feasible in cases (like those of children) where the consequences are manageable. Such a strategy may not be helpful for those whose behavior is too destructive or unmanageable.

The case of Jane, then, demonstrates a less traditional application of a therapeutic strategy for paradox-analytic purposes. The basis for Jane's problem was one of hyperexpansion. Because of several acute traumas (i.e., male "abandonments"), she had become, in paradox-analytic terms, deathly afraid of "disappearing" and did all she could to *manifest* herself. The aim of Jane's treatment, accordingly, was to help her optimize her capacity to constrict. This was accomplished, eventually, by inviting Jane to observe her own folly. After enough cheating and winning she became saturated. She no longer needed to glorify herself. She no longer needed to expand at all costs. By contrast, she began to see the value of *channeling* her energies, and thereby increasing her safety, enjoyment, and general effectiveness.

Sally: A Case of Hyperconstriction

A 45-year-old married woman whom I shall call Sally stepped into my office one early March evening. She was tearful, downcast, and tense. She told me that she had just undergone surgery for the removal of a benign tumor, and that she didn't know what was happening to her.

In reviewing her history, it soon became clear that Sally had undergone much more than surgery—she had undergone an intense and long-standing sense of victimization. Although Sally reported feeling "fine" the last eight years, her self-characterizations belied that claim.

Sally's earliest memories, vague though they were, suggested that she was an ordinary, lively child. However, at age seven, her world came crashing down. Her mother contracted and quickly died of a kidney ailment, and Sally and her five siblings were relocated to their aunt, who allegedly resented the "burden." Two short years later Sally's father, who was reportedly a drug addict and drifter, also died. These two blows, coupled with a "mean and cruel" aunt, devastated Sally. She began to withdraw from other children and become increasingly reserved, shy, and self-deprecating.

Sally apparently "managed" like this through the balance of her childhood, and even the early part of her marriage. However, she did report feeling suicidal and overdosing on "diet" pills for a short period toward the beginning of her marriage. The reason she gave for this episode was that she was miserable and wanted to escape, but she did not elaborate further.

My early work with Sally centered on clarifying her needs, motives, and intentions. This helped us both get a better grip on her "world-design," as Binswanger might put it. What emerged from this endeavor was that Sally felt a great deal of impotency about her life, and was very fearful of changing. Her helplessness was especially marked in relation to her career interests and goals and to her husband. With regard to her career, Sally was directionless. She had some interest in medical technology, and a vocational degree in that area, but was afraid to pursue it, afraid that she would fail, or would find it uninteresting.

Sally's husband, moreover, had a history of cocaine abuse, and a corresponding history of being "obnoxious," or reckless when "high." Although Sally detested his behavior at such times, she went along with his justifications, and often just denied the issue. By the time Sally entered my office, however, it was clear that she could not go on denying. Her surgery had signaled to her that she could no longer tolerate rampant victimization in her life, and had to seek alternatives.

The early stages of my work with Sally were marked by "exercises" and gradual attempts to help her see her "larger self," as I put it. I used cognitive reframing to help Sally see how her thinking was restricting her. For example, I questioned her assumption that she "just couldn't" assert herself with a colleague (at a hospital in which she was a volunteer). We examined the implications of that self-imposed stricture, such as the fact that it ran counter to behavior she had demonstrated in the past, and that it totally negated her ability to make choices. We also looked at "worst-case" scenarios. What's the worst that could happen if she stood up to her peer, we queried. She would then trace out her fantasy, which was often much less wretched than she at first feared.

Reflecting back to Sally her reactions also facilitated cognitive reframing. Such mirroring helped her to see the folly in her assertions, or to "hear" otherwise "silent" capabilities, such as potentially constructive anger or excitement.

I further recommended that Sally begin to become aware of inhibited moments. I asked her to note them and to begin sorting her inhibited feelings from what actually was likely to take place in a given situation. For example, she perceived her antagonistic peer like her tyrannical aunt in many ways. Recognition of this helped her to separate, and thus alleviate, the projection from her past (i.e., horror of her aunt) from the concern at present (i.e., frustration with a condescending coworker). Similarly, such sorting helped her to strip away her idealization of her husband whom she was "enabling" to abuse drugs. Once she acknowledged her projection of him as the father she never had (recall that her father, too, was an addict), she was more able to set appropriate limits with him.

Although these behavioral and "insight-oriented" strategies helped for a time, it became clear that they only superficially alleviated Sally's depression. The more Sally confronted *fundamental* changes, such as taking a consequential stand with her husband about his drug abuse or embarking on a career change, the less technical skills helped her cope (see Bugental, 1978, on the relative commonality of this sequence). She needed and appeared capable of *affective* expansion.

Accordingly, I began orienting my work with Sally toward the "process" or "nonverbal" aspects of her awareness. Gradually, I prodded her to begin *experiencing* her fears of asserting herself with others, rather than merely reporting those fears. I did this partly through my own responses to her. For example, I took a stance with her that allowed little intellectualizing. I would point out to her when she appeared to be "coming from her head," and when it was that I (demonstrably) felt her emotional resonance with a given topic.

One of the most important things I learned from my own therapy, I told her, was the ability to "stay with my feelings." I used an analogy that I've fostered over the years. Despair is like plunging into a pitch-black basement in which many sharp and obstructing objects have been stored. Instantly, you panic and don't know what to do. There are so many potentially dangerous items around almost beckoning to inflict pain!

Yet one of the things that begins to happen if you do not get carried away with yourself and charge recklessly about, or withdraw into a deep despondency, is that you become familiar with your surroundings. Slowly, your eyes adjust to the minimal light, and the contours of objects begin to form. A desk there, an old hat here, a lamp that you thought was a man-eating bug. Gradually, fretful noises turn into familiar sounds—the crash of an old coffee cup, the whisk of a shirt on a musty clothes line. You begin stumbling your way through, and to your surprise, not only are objects beginning to feel familiar, they are beginning to interest you. There's the old photo album you stashed away so many years ago, and the silver medal you won at that track meet. Oh, and there's the place that your brother slept; it is covered with cobwebs now, but remember all those rough and tumble times you used to have together? And yes, that fishing pole has a sharp hook on the end of it, but it also brings back the time you had that "heart to heart" with Uncle Henry on Sea Bass Bay.

My point here is that as we begin to listen as opposed to judge, as we begin to look as opposed to scheme, we begin to discover the patchworks of life, not necessarily the nightmares we build (or built) life up to be. Thus, what I was trying to convey to Sally was a form of becoming aware of herself, so well described by Bugental (1976). It is the art of "staying with" and becoming familiar with the feeling tone of one's concerns (in this case experiences which demand expansiveness), thereby feeling less threatened by those concerns. The second result is that one becomes more "centered" in one's needs, wants, and life-circumstances, and better able to take effective action regarding them.

The more we can help clients like Sally in this way, the more adaptive such clients can be in a multiplicity of situations. This is because centric (or intrinsic) perception is not susceptible to the disturbances that environmentally (or extrinsically) oriented perception is susceptible to. When we, as individuals, are in control of our outlook, the chances for decompensation are relatively small. On the other hand, when we must depend on others or a behaviorally designed environment to control us, the chances for decompensation appear to increase markedly (Green, Wilson, & Lovato, 1986).

Continuing our discussion of Sally, then, my thrust at this stage was to help her look more closely at the emotional aspects of her constrictedness. We examined pertinent situations, such as taking a stand with her husband concerning his drug abuse. We enlivened such situations through rehearsal, role-playing, and gentle prompts for her to "stay with" herself while engaging these tasks. She described herself as feeling "weak," "insignificant," "helpless," "girlish," "wimpy," and "trapped." Yet as she pursued the tasks, she felt increasingly bold about actually confronting her husband and others with whom she felt needlessly stifled. She began to see that her small, helpless feelings related to her past, or to a facade that she no longer felt justified in holding up. She was tired of playing the victim role, and was ready to assume the advantages of taking increased responsibility for her problems, risky though that might be. At the same time, Sally became increasingly aware of her anger toward feeling oppressed, and saw that she could use it constructively.

Correspondingly, Sally started on a path of increased self-acceptance and assertiveness. She proceeded to find a paid job in a hospital, signed up for art classes, and scheduled a weekly breakfast with a good friend. Moreover, she reported feeling less intimidated by people and less concerned with what they thought of her. She also reported feeling less critical of herself and more able to express her needs to people.

This rejuvenated attitude came to a head one late afternoon at home. Sally walked up to her husband and told him that she could no longer tolerate his drug addiction. She insisted that he join a local self-help group and that he refrain from ingesting cocaine. Her husband was reportedly frustrated by her demands but reluctantly agreed to join the group. He did not, however, agree to refrain from drug-taking until she conveyed to him an ultimatum: "Either you stop 'snorting coke' or I will take the children and leave."

Despite Sally's presentation of the ultimatum to her

husband, she was quite ambivalent about it. She spent a great deal of time in therapy trying to determine if, indeed, she was willing to carry it out. Eventually, she decided she would.

My work with Sally ended sooner than both of us would have liked (due to my departure from our assigned clinic). Nevertheless, our exchange for one and a half years yielded, she and I believed, fruitful results. Sally's husband apparently refrained from drug-taking after her ultimatum (which was several months before therapy terminated). He was, however, erratic about attending the chemical dependency group. The two of them also agreed to go to marital counseling to work out their growing discontent. Finally, Sally began the process of searching out enhanced career prospects, such as a nursing degree program.

In short, Sally learned to *expand* her capabilities by reframing her thoughts and familiarizing herself with her feelings. She realized that many of her impediments were her own, spurred on by chronic childhood stresses and an entrenched lifestyle. She began to see what many who step out into the light of self-acceptance see—that daunting shadows can recede.

This concludes our discussion of paradox-analysis. The key dictums here have been (1) address the client's desire and capacity for (constrictive or expansive) integration; (2) align the therapeutic approach with this desire and capacity; and (3) invite clients into increasingly anxious domains of their experience (keeping fully aware of the first dictum), so as to enhance their capacity to constructively transform those domains. I hope that I have shown how therapeutically vital are these little rules.

CONCLUSION

This book is an opening statement. It is a preliminary attempt to consider what paradox is, how it affects us, and what we can do about it. We began with the writings of Kierkegaard and on that basis developed a model of human functioning—the paradox principle. The paradox principle holds that the psyche is a constrictive/expansive continuum, only degrees of which are conscious. Constriction is the perceived "drawing back" and confinement of thoughts, feelings, and sensations; expansion is the perceived "bursting forth" and extension of thoughts, feelings, and sensations. Constrictive consciousness is characterized by yielding and focusing elements; expansive consciousness is marked by asserting and incorporating elements.

One's center or centric mode is the capacity to be aware of and direct one's constrictive and expansive potentialities.

Finally, *dread* of constrictive or expansive polarities promotes dysfunction, extremism, or polarization; appropriate *confrontation* with, or integration of, the poles fosters optimal living.

To what extent was the paradox principle upheld by empirical evidence? After reviewing data in the areas of psychological dysfunctions, "health," and psychotherapy, it can safely be concluded that it does support the model, and suggests the need for further investigation.

We have found, for example, that dysfunctional behavior reflects a wide range of constrictive and expansive extremes, that some of these extremes are due to various forms of trauma, and that trauma itself is due to (constrictive or expansive) extremes that are perceived to oppose one or one's group.

We have also found that optimal people (and moments) are characterized by a capacity to confront constrictive and expansive polarities, transform them, and use them productively—to enhance creativity, physical health, organizations, communities, child-raising, and religious commitments.

Finally, we have found that people can learn to integrate constrictive and expansive polarities therapeutically through simple behavioral techniques, cognitive exercises, intense self-observation, and many other approaches. The pivotal issues are the client's desire and capacity for change, and how best to meet that desire and capacity.

We are thus beset by this elastic mindscape called the paradox principle. The psyche that has emerged out of our analysis is a divided one. It is a consciousness marked by tension, extremes, and sometimes elegant proportion. It is not the psyche of psychoanalysis, although it is kindred in many ways and attempts to broaden that standpoint. Likewise, it is not the psyche of holistic or transpersonal psychology, although it acknowledges transcendence.

The paradoxical mind, by contrast, moves *toward* the infinite (or immortal), but also justifiably recoils at the prospect. It strives for fullness, completion, omnipotence. And yet it is horrified by the implications of this prompting.

It is horrified to sense that at the "ends" of the infinite continuum is a maddening microcosm and macrocosm—a psychic black hole, where experiences dissolve at their respective horizons and the world is no longer recognizable.

The key questions of this book accordingly are: To what extent does one recoil from infinitude? To what extent does one embrace/integrate it?

These questions lead to religious concerns. What are the parameters one sets around one's life? How much action and experience does one permit within those parameters? At what point does one give up one's searching and surrender to the powers that be? In short, how far does one push one's "God," whether that deity is a 9-to-5 job, a spouse, a project, or a traditional form of worship? These, indeed, as Becker enjoins us, are the burning problems for psychotherapy and psychology.

REFERENCES

Abramson, J. (1984). *Liberation and its limits. The moral and political thought of Freud.* Boston: Beacon Press.

Achenbach, T. (1982). *Developmental psychopathology.* New York: Wiley.

Adler, A. (1927). *The practice and theory of individual psychology.* New York: Harcourt Brace Jovanovich.

Adorno, T., Frenkel-Brunswick, E., Levinson, D., & Sanford, R. (1950). *The authoritarian personality.* New York: Harper & Row.

Agheana, I. (1984). *The prose of Jorge Luis Borges: Existentialism and the dynamics of surprise.* New York: Peter Lang.

Allport, G. (1979). *The nature of prejudice.* Reading, MA: Addison-Wesley.

American Psychiatric Association. (1980). *Diagnostic and statistical manual of mental disorders* (3d ed.). Washington DC: American Psychiatric Association.

Andrews, J. (1966). Psychotherapy of phobias. *Psychological Bulletin, 66,* 455–480.

Antonovsky, A. (1979). *Health, stress, and coping.* San Francisco: Jossey-Bass.

Arcaya, J. (1979). A phenomenology of fear. *Journal of Phenomenological Psychology, 10,* 165–188.

Arieti, S. (1974). *Interpretation of schizophrenia.* New York: Basic Books.

Arieti, S. (1976). *Creativity: The magic synthesis.* New York: Basic Books.

Arieti, S. (1981). The family of the schizophrenic and its participation in the therapeutic task. In S. Arieti and H. Brodie (Eds.), *American handbook of psychiatry: Advances and new directions* (Vol. 7, pp. 271–284). New York: Basic Books.

Aron, E. & Aron, A. (1987). The influence of inner state on self-reported long-term happiness. *Journal of Humanistic Psychology, 27* (2), 248–270.

Asher, J. (1987, April). Born to be shy. *Psychology Today*, pp. 56–64.

Avishai, B. (1985). *The tragedy of Zionism.* New York: Farrar, Strauss, & Giroux.

Bandura, A. (1977). *Social learning theory.* Englewood Cliffs, NJ: Prentice-Hall.

Barrett, W. (1978). *The illusion of technique.* New York: Anchor Books.

Barron, F. (1963). *Creativity and psychological health.* New York: Van Nostrand.

Bateson, G., Jackson, D., Haley, J., & Weakland, J. (1956). Toward a theory of schizophrenia. *Behavioral Sciences, 1,* 251–264.

Baumrind, D. (1971). Current patterns of parental authority. *Developmental Psychology Monograph, 4* (1), 1–103.

Beck, A. (1976). *Cognitive therapy and the emotional disorders.* New York: Signet.

Becker, E. (1973). *Denial of death.* New York: Free Press.

Becker, E. (1975). *Escape from evil.* New York: Free Press.

Becker, E. (1982). Growing up rugged: Fritz Perls and gestalt therapy. *Revision, 5* (2), 6–14.

Bellah, R., Madsen, R., Sullivan, M., Swidler, A., & Tipton, S. (1985). *Habits of the heart.* New York: Perennial Library.

Benedict, R. (1934). *Patterns of culture.* Boston: Houghton Mifflin.

Benson, H. (1979). The relaxation response: Techniques and applications. In D. Sobel (Ed.), *Ways of health* (pp. 331–351). New York: Harcourt Brace Jovanovich.

Bergin, A. & Lambert, M. (1978). The evaluation of therapeutic outcomes. In S. Garfield & A. Bergin (Eds.), *Handbook of psychotherapy and behavior change: An empirical analysis* (pp. 139–190). New York: Wiley.

Berman, M. (1989). The roots of reality. Maturana and Varela's *The Tree of Knowledge. Journal of Humanistic Psychology, 29* (2), 277–284.

Bettelheim, B. (1960). *The informed heart: Autonomy in a mass age.* Glencoe, IL: Free Press.

Bharati, A. (1976). *The light at the center: The context and pretext of modern mysticism.* Santa Barbara: CA: Ross-Erickson.

Binswanger, L. (1958a). The existential analysis school of thought (E. Angel, Trans.). In R. May, E. Angel, & H. Ellenberger (Eds.),

Existence: A new dimension in psychiatry and psychology. (pp. 191–213). New York: Basic Books. (Original work published in 1946.)

Binswanger, L. (1958b). The case of Ellen West (W. Mendel and J. Lyons, Trans.). In R. May, E. Angel, & H. Ellenberger (Eds.), *Existence: A new dimension in psychiatry and psychology* (pp. 237–364). New York: Basic Books. (Original work published in 1945.)

Binswanger, L. (1975). *Being in the world: Selected papers of Ludwig Binswanger.* (J. Needleman, Trans.) New York: Basic Books.

Bowen, M. (1978). *Family therapy in clinical practice.* New York: Jason Aronson.

Bowers, M. & Freedman, D. (1972). "Psychedelic" experiences in acute psychoses. In C. Tart (Ed.), *Altered states of consciousness* (pp. 473–487). New York: Anchor/Doubleday.

Brown, D. (1977). A model for the levels of concentrative meditation. *The International Journal of Clinical and Experimental Hypnosis, 25* (4), 236–273.

Buber, M. (1965). *The knowledge of man: A philosophy of the interhuman.* (M. Friedman & R. Smith, Trans.). New York: Harper & Row.

Buber, M. (1967). *On Judaism.* New York: Schocken Books.

Bugental, J. (1976). *The search for existential identity.* San Francisco: Jossey-Bass.

Bugental, J. (1978). *Psychotherapy and Process.* Reading, MA: Addison-Wesley.

Bugental, J. (1981). *The search for authenticity: An existential-analytic approach to psychotherapy.* New York: Irvington.

Cameron, N. (1963). *Personality development and psychopathology.* Boston: Houghton Mifflin.

Campbell, R. (1988, May 29). Regulation shouldn't bar creativity. *Boston Globe,* p. B-10.

Campbell, S. (1980). *The couple's journey: Intimacy as a path to wholeness.* San Luis Obispo, CA: Impact.

Campbell, S. (1983). *Earth community: Living experiments in cultural transformation.* San Francisco: Evolutionary Press.

Cannon, W. (1929). *Bodily changes in pain, hunger, fear, and rage.* New York: Appleton.

Carnegie Corporation Staff. (1961, July). Creativity. *Carnegie Corporation of New York Quarterly,* pp. 1–7.

Charlesworth, E. & Nathan, R. (1982). *Stress management: A comprehensive guide to wellness.* New York: Ballantine.

Chernin, K. (1981). *The obsession: Reflections on the tyranny of slenderness*. New York: Harper & Row.

Coleman, J. (1976). *Abnormal psychology and modern life*. Glenview, IL: Scott, Foresman.

Corrington, R. (1987). Hermeneutics and psychopathology: Jaspers and Hillman. *Theoretical and Philosophical Psychology, 7* (2), 70–80.

Craig, E. (1988). Daseinsanalysis: A quest for essentials. In E. Craig (Ed.), *Psychotherapy for freedom: The Daseinsanalytic way in psychology and psychoanalysis. A special issue of The Humanistic Psychologist, 16* (1), pp. 1–21.

Deleuze, G. & Guattari, F. (1977). *Anti-Oedipus: Capitalism and schizophrenia*. New York: Viking-Penguin.

Drevdahl, J. (1964). Some developmental and environmental factors in creativity. In C. Taylor (Ed.), *Widening horizons in creativity* (pp. 176–186). New York: Wiley.

Eisenstadt, M. (1978, March). Parental loss and genius. *American Psychologist*, pp. 211–223.

Eisler, R. (1987). *The chalice and the blade: Our history, our future*. San Francisco: Harper & Row.

Elkind, D. (1987, May) Superkids and superproblems. *Psychology Today*, pp. 60–61.

Ellenberger, H. (1958). A clinical introduction to psychiatric phenomenology and existential analysis. In R. May, E. Angel, and H. Ellenberger (Eds.), *Existence: A new dimension in psychiatry and psychology* (pp. 92–124). New York: Basic Books.

Ellis, A. (1962). *Reason and emotion in psychotherapy*. New York: Lyle Stuart.

Emde, R. (1985). *Early identification of children at risk: An international perspective*. New York: Plenum.

Erikson, E. (1963). *Childhood and society*. New York: Norton.

Erikson, E. (1975). *Life history and the historical moment*. New York: Norton.

Exner, J. (1986). *The Rorschach: A comprehensive system, basic foundations* (Vol. I). New York: Wiley.

Eysenck, H. (1957). *The dynamics of anxiety and hysteria*. New York: Praeger.

Farson, R. (1974). *Birthrights*. New York: Macmillan.

Faulconer, J. & Williams, R. (1985). Temporality in human action: An alternative to positivism and historicism. *American Psychologist, 40* (11), 1179–1188.

Fieve, R. (1975). *Moodswing: The third revolution in psychiatry.* New York: Morrow.

Fisher, S. & Greenberg, R. (1985). *The scientific credibility of Freud's theories and therapy.* New York: Columbia University Press.

FitzGerald, F. (1986a, September 22). Rajneeshpuram I. *The New Yorker,* pp. 45–94.

FitzGerald, F. (1986b, September 29). Rajneeshpuram II. *The New Yorker,* pp. 83–126.

Foucault, M. (1965). *Madness and civilization: A history of insanity in the age of reason* (R. Howard, Trans.). New York: Vintage. (Original work published in 1961.)

Frank, J. (1973). *Persuasion and healing: A comparative study of psychotherapy.* Baltimore: Johns Hopkins University Press.

Frankl, V. (1969). *The will to meaning.* Cleveland: New American Library.

Franz, M. von (1975). *C.G. Jung: His myth in our time* (W. Kennedy, Trans.). Boston: Little Brown. (Original work published in 1972.)

Freud, S. (1958). The dynamics of transference. In J. Strachey (Ed.), *The standard edition of the complete works of Sigmund Freud* (Vol. 12, pp. 97–108). London: Hogarth Press. (Original work published in 1912.)

Freud, S. (1961). The ego and the id. In J. Strachey (Ed. and Trans.), *The standard edition of the complete psychological works of Sigmund Freud* (Vol. 19, pp. 3–66). London: Hogarth Press. (Original work published in 1923.)

Freud, S. (1963). *A general introduction to psychoanalysis* (J. Riviere, Trans.). New York: Pocket Books. (Original work published in 1920.)

Freud, S. (1966). Civilization and its discontents. In J. Strachey (Ed.), *The complete psychological works of Sigmund Freud* (Vol. 21, pp. 59–145). London: Hogarth Press. (Original work published in 1930.)

Friedman, H. & Booth-Kewley, S. (1987). The "disease-prone" personality: A meta-analytic view of the construct. *American Psychologist, 42* (6), 539–555.

Freidman, M. & Rosenman, R. (1974). *Type A behavior and your heart.* Greenwich, CT: Fawcett.

Fromm, E. (1947). *Man for himself.* New York: Holt, Rinehart & Winston.

Fromm, E. (1950). *Psychoanalysis and religion.* New Haven: Yale University Press.

Fromm, E. (1956). *The art of loving.* New York: Harper & Row.

Fromm, E. (1965). *Escape from freedom.* New York: Holt, Rinehart & Winston.

Fromm, E. (1973). *The anatomy of human destructiveness.* New York: Holt, Rinehart & Winston.

Garfield, C. (1986). *Peak performers: The new heroes of American business.* New York: Avon.

Gendlin, E. (1978). *Focusing.* New York: Bantam.

Gebsattel, V. von (1958). The world of the compulsive (S. Koppel & E. Angel, Trans.). In R. May, E. Angel, & H. Ellenberger (Eds.), *Existence: A new dimension in psychiatry and psychology* (pp. 170–187). New York: Basic Books.

Ghadirian, A. & Engelsmann, F. (1985). Somatic illness in manic-depressive and schizophrenic patients. *Journal of Psychosomatic Research, 29* (3), 281–286.

Gilligan, C. (1982). *In a different voice: Psychological theory and women's development.* Cambridge: Harvard University Press.

Giorgi, A. (1970). *Psychology as a human science: A phenomenologically based approach.* New York: Harper & Row.

Giorgi, A. (1987). The crisis of humanistic psychology. *Humanistic Psychologist, 15,* (1), 5–20.

Goertzel, V. & Goertzel, M. (1962). *Cradles of eminence.* Boston: Little, Brown.

Goffman, I. (1959). *The presentation of self in everyday life.* New York: Doubleday/Anchor.

Goldfried, M.R. (Ed.) (1982). *Converging themes in psychotherapy: Trends in psychodynamic, humanistic, and behavioral practice.* New York: Springer.

Goodkin, K., Antoni, M., & Blaney, P. (1986). Stress and hopelessness in the promotion of cervical intraepithelial neoplasia to invasive squamous cell carcinoma of the cervix. *Journal of Psychosomatic Research, 30* (1), 67–76.

Graetz, H. (1963). *The symbolic language of Vincent Van Gogh.* New York: McGraw-Hill.

Grant, V. (1968). *Great abnormals.* New York: Hawthorne.

Green, L., Wilson, A., & Lovato, C. (1986). What changes can health promotion achieve and how long do these changes last? The trade-offs between expediency and durability. *Preventive Medicine, 15,* 508–521.

Gruber, H. (1984). *Darwin on man: A psychological study of scientific creativity*. Chicago: University of Chicago Press.

Guntrip, H. (1969). *Schizoid phenomena, object relations, and the self*. New York: International Universities Press.

Hamilton, A., Madison, J., & Jay, J. (1982). *The federalist papers*. New York: Bantam Books. (Original work published in 1787–1788.)

Hampden-Turner, C. (1970). *Radical man: The process of psychosocial development*. Cambridge, MA: Schenkman.

Heelas, P., & Lock, A. (Eds.). (1981). *Indigenous psychologies: The anthropology of the self*. London: Academic Press.

Heidegger, M. (1962). *Being and time*. New York: Harper & Row.

Herzberg, F., Mausner, B., & Snyderman, B. (1959). *The motivation to work*. New York: Wiley.

Hoffer, E. (1951). *The true believer*. New York: Harper & Row.

Holden, C. (1987, April) Creativity and the troubled mind. *Psychology Today*, pp. 9–10.

Horney, K. (1939). *New ways in psychoanalysis*. New York: Norton.

House, R. (1971). A path-goal theory of leader effectiveness. *Administrative Science Quarterly, 2*, 321–339.

Husserl, E. (1931). *Ideas: General introduction to pure phenomenology* (W. Gibson, Trans.). New York: Macmillan.

Huxley, A. (1956). *The doors of perception and heaven and hell*. New York: Harper & Row.

James, W. (1963). *Pragmatism and other essays*. New York: Washington Square Press. (Most of original work published in 1910.)

Janos, P. & Robinson, N. (1985). Psychosocial development in intellectually gifted children. In F. Horowitz & M. O'Brian (Eds.), *The gifted and talented: Developmental perspectives* (pp. 149–187). Washington DC: American Psychological Association.

Jaspers, K. (1963) *General psychopathology* (J. Hoenig and M. Hamilton, Trans.). Chicago: University of Chicago Press. (Original work published in 1913.)

Johnston, M. (Ed.) (1967). *The cosmos of Arthur Holly Compton*. New York: Knopf.

Jones, E. (1981). *The life and work of Sigmund Freud* (Vol. 1). New York: Basic Books. (Original work published in 1953.)

Jourard, S. (1968). *Disclosing man to himself*. New York: Van Nostrand.

Jourard, S. (1971). *The transparent self*. New York: Van Nostrand.

Jung, C. (1958). *Psyche and symbol: A selection from the writings of C.G. Jung* (V. Laszlo, Ed.). Garden City, NY: Anchor/Doubleday.

Jung, C. (1963). *Memories, dreams, and reflections* (R. Winston & C. Winston, Trans.) New York: Vintage.

Jung, C. (1966). *Two essays on analytical psychology* (R. Hull, Trans.). Princeton, NJ: Princeton University Press. (Original work published in 1928 and 1943.)

Jung, C. (1974). *Dreams* (R. Hull, Trans.). Princeton, NJ: Princeton University Press.

Kant, I. (1929). *Critique of pure reason* (N. Smith, Trans.). London: Macmillan.

Kaufmann, W. (1968). *Nietzsche: Philosopher, psychologist, antichrist.* New York: Vintage Books.

Kazdin, A. (1978). The application of operant techniques in treatment, rehabilitation, and education. In A. Bergin and S. Garfield (Eds.), *Handbook of psychotherapy and behavior change: An empirical analysis* (pp. 549–589). New York: Wiley.

Khantzian, E.J. (1985). The self-medication hypothesis of addictive disorders: Focus on heroin and cocaine dependence. *The American Journal of Psychiatry, 142* (11), 1259–1264.

Kiekolt-Glaser, J., Stephens, R., Lipetz, P., Speicher, C., & Glaser, R. (1985). Distress and DNA repair in human lymphocytes. *Journal of Behavioral Medicine, 8* (4), 391–404.

Kierkegaard, S. (1954). *Fear and trembling and sickness unto death* (W. Lowrie, Trans.). Princeton, NJ: Princeton University Press. (Original works published in 1843 and 1849.)

King, M. (1969). Letter from Birmingham jail. In A. Eastman (Ed.), *The Norton reader: An anthology of expository prose* (pp. 556–570). New York: Norton.

Klein, D. (1972). *Psychiatric case studies: Treatment, drugs, and outcome.* Baltimore: Williams & Wilkins.

Klein, G. (1976). *Psychoanalytic theory: The exploration of essentials.* New York: International Universities Press.

Kobasa, S. (1979). Stressful life events, personality and health: An inquiry into hardiness. *Journal of Personality and Social Psychology, 37*, 1–11.

Kobasa, S., Maddi, S., & Puccetti, M. (1982). Personality and exercise as buffers in the stress-illness relationship. *Journal of Behavioral Medicine, 5* (4), 391–404.

Kobasa, S., Maddi, S., & Zola, M. (1983). Type A and hardiness. *Journal of Behavioral Medicine, 6* (1), 41–51.

Kohut, H. (1977). *The restoration of the self.* New York: International Universities Press.

Kohut, H. (1985). *Self psychology and the humanities: Reflections on a new psychoanalytic approach.* New York: Norton.

Krippner, S. & Dillard, J. (1988). *Dreamworking: How to use your dreams for creative problem solving.* New York: Bearly Limited.

Kris, E. (1952). *Psychoanalytic explorations in art.* New York: International Universities Press.

Kuhn, R. (1958). The attempted murder of a prostitute (E. Angel, Trans.). In R. May, E. Angel, & H. Ellenberger (Eds.), *Existence: A new dimension in psychiatry and psychology* (pp. 365–425). New York: Basic Books. (Original work published in 1948.)

Kuhn, T. (1970). *The structure of scientific revolutions.* Chicago: University of Chicago Press.

Laing, R. (1961). *Self and others.* Middlesex, England: Penguin.

Laing, R. (1967). *Politics of experience.* New York: Ballantine.

Laing, R. (1969). *The divided self: An existential study in sanity and madness.* Middlesex, England: Penguin.

Laing, R. (1971). *The politics of the family and other essays.* New York: Vintage.

Laing, R. (1985). *Wisdom, madness, & folly: The making of a psychiatrist.* New York: McGraw-Hill.

Lange-Eichbaum, W. (1932). *The problem of genius* (E. Paul & C. Paul, Trans.). New York: Macmillan.

Lasch, C. (1979). *The culture of narcissism.* New York: Norton.

Lee, D. (1959). *Freedom and culture.* Englewood Cliffs, NJ: Prentice-Hall.

Leo, J. (1984, October). The ups and downs of creativity: Genius and emotional disturbance are linked in a new study. *Time*, p. 76.

Lifton, R. (1969). *Boundaries: Psychological man in revolution.* New York: Vintage.

Lifton, R. (1976). *The life of the self.* New York: Basic Books.

Linville, P. (1987). Self-complexity as a cognitive buffer against stress-related illness and depression. *Journal of Personality and Social Psychology, 52* (4), 663–676.

Lombroso, C. (1910). *The man of genius.* New York: Scribner.

Lowen, A. (1970). The body in therapy. *American Dance Therapy Association Proceedings* (Fifth Annual Conference), pp. 1–9.

Lyketsos, G. & Lyketsos, C. (1986). Hostility and mind-body interactions: A Greek perspective. *Advances, 3* (4), 122–133.

MacDonald, N. (1979). Living with schizophrenia. In D. Goleman & R. Davidson (Eds.), *Consciousness: Brain, states of awareness, and mysticism* (pp. 111–114). New York: Harper & Row.

Maddi, S. (1976). *Personality theories.* Homewood IL: Dorsey.

Maher, A. & Nadler, W. (1986). Good moments in psychotherapy: A preliminary review, a list, and some promising research avenues. *Journal of Consulting and Clinical Psychology 54* (1), 10–15.

Marks, I. (1978). Behavior therapy of adult neurosis. In S. Garfield & A. Bergin (Eds.), *Handbook of psychotherapy and behavior change: An empirical analysis* (pp. 493–547). New York: Wiley.

Masek, R. (1986). Self-psychology as psychology: The revision of Heinz Kohut. *Theoretical and Philosophical Psychology, 6* (1), 22–30.

Maslow, A. (1968). *Toward a psychology of being.* New York: Van Nostrand.

Maslow, A. (1971). *The farther reaches of human nature.* New York: Penguin.

May, R. (1958a). The origins and significance of the existential movement in psychology. In R. May, E. Angel, and H. Ellenberger (Eds.), *Existence: A new dimension in psychiatry and psychology* (pp. 3–36). New York: Basic Books.

May, R. (1958b). Contributions of existential psychotherapy. In R. May, E. Angel, and H. Ellenberger (Eds.), *Existence: A new dimension in psychiatry and psychology* (pp. 37–91). New York: Basic Books.

May, R. (1969). *Love and will.* New York: Norton.

May, R. (1977). *The meaning of anxiety.* New York: Pocket Books.

May, R. (1981). *Freedom and destiny.* New York: Norton.

May, R. (1985). *My quest for beauty.* Dallas, TX: Saybrook.

McClelland, D., Ross, G., & Patel, V. (1985). The effect of academic examination on salivary norepinephrine and immunoglobulin levels. *Journal of Human Stress, 11*, 52–59.

McDevitt, J. & Mahler, M. (1980). Object constancy, individuality, and internalization. In S. Greenspan & G. Pollock (Eds.), *The course of life: Psychoanalytic contributions toward understanding personality development* (Vol. 1, pp. 407–423). Washington DC: National Institute of Mental Health.

McGoldrick, M. & Gerson, R. (1985). *Genograms in family assessment.* New York: Norton.

Merleau-Ponty, M. (1962). *Phenomenology of perception.* London: Routledge & Kegan Paul.

Merleau-Ponty, M. (1963). *The Structure of behavior.* Boston: Beacon Press.

Meyerhoff, M. & White, B. (1986, September). Making the grade as parents. *Psychology Today*, pp. 38–45.

Miller, A. (1981). *The drama of the gifted child* (R. Ward, Trans.). New York: Basic Books. (Original work published in 1979.)

Miller, W., Rosellini, R., & Seligman, M. (1977). Learned helplessness and depression. In J. Maser & M. Seligman (Eds.), *Psychopathology: Experimental models* (pp. 104–130). San Francisco: W.H. Freeman.

Millon, T. (1981). *Disorders of personality: DSM III, Axis II*. New York: Wiley.

Moyers, B. (1988, March 28). [Interview with Phillip Hallie in Public Affairs Television Program, *Facing Evil*—a conference sponsored by the Institute for the Humanities]. *Journal Graphics*, New York, NY. This typescript has also been published as a book: *Facing Evil: light at the core of darkness*, P. Woodruff and H. Wilmer (Eds.) (1988), LaSalle, IL. Open Court.

Muzika, E. (1988, June 2). *Object relations theory, introspection, and the self: A phenomenological synthesis of Eastern and Western approaches*. Paper presented at the University of California, Los Angeles.

Needleman, J. (1975). The symbol in psychoanalysis and daseinsanalyse. In L. Binswanger (J. Needleman, Trans.), *Being in the world: Selected papers of Ludwig Binswanger* (pp. 59–83). New York: Basic Books.

Norcross, J. (1986). Eclectic psychotherapy: An introduction and overview. In J. Norcross (Ed.), *Handbook of eclectic psychotherapy* (pp. 1–22). New York: Brunner/Mazel.

O'Hara, M. (1985). Comment on Carl Rogers' "Toward a more human science of the person." *Journal of Humanistic Psychology, 25* (4), 25–30.

Ornstein, R. & Sobel, D. (1987, March). The healing brain. *Psychology Today*, pp. 48–52.

Pahnke, W. & Richards, W. (1972). Implications of LSD and experimental mysticism. In C. Tart (Ed.), *Altered states of consciousness* (pp. 409–439). New York: Anchor Books.

Parks, C., Benjamin, B., & Fitzgerald, R. (1969). Broken heart: A statistical study of increased mortality among widowers. *British Medical Journal, 1*, 740–743.

Patterson, G. (1986). Performance models for antisocial boys. *American Psychologist, 41* (4), 432–444.

Pearl, C. (1984, July 12). The perils of zealotry. *The Jerusalem Post*, p. 8.

Peters, T. & Waterman, R. (1982). *In search of excellence*. New York: Harper & Row.

Piaget, J. (1971). *The theory of stages in cognitive development*. In D. Green, M. Ford, & G. Flamer (Eds.), *Measurement and Piaget* (pp. 1–11). New York: McGraw-Hill.

Prentky, R. (1979). Creativity and psychopathology: A neurocognitive perspective. In B. Maher (Ed.), *Progress in experimental personality research* (pp. 1–39). New York: Academic Press.

Quinn, J. (1985, May–June). Managing innovation: Controlled chaos: *Harvard Business Review*, pp. 73–84.

Rank, O. (1936). *Will therapy* (J. Taft, Trans.). New York: Knopf. (Original work published in 1929.)

Rank, O. (1941). *Beyond psychology*. New York: Dover.

Rank, O. (1968). *Art and artist*. New York: Agathon Press. (Original work published in 1932.)

Richards, R. (1981). Relationships between creativity and psychopathology: An evaluation and interpretation of the evidence. *Genetic Psychology Monographs, 103*, 261–324.

Richardson, R. (1986). *Henry Thoreau: A life of the mind*. Berkeley, CA: University of California Press.

Riegel, K. (1976). The dialectics of human development. *American Psychologist, 31*, 689–699.

Rogers, C. (1985). Toward a more human science of the person. *Journal of Humanistic Psychology, 25* (4), 7–24.

Rokeach, M. (1960). *The open and closed mind*. New York: Basic Books.

Rorty, R. (1979). *Philosophy and the mirror of nature*. Princeton, NJ: Princeton University Press.

Rothenberg, A. (1979). *The emerging goddess: The creative process in art, science, and other fields*. Chicago: University of Chicago Press.

Royce, J. (1964). *The encapsulated man*. New York: Van Nostrand Reinhold.

Rutan, J. (1987, April 18). *Making of a supervisor: The teaching and learning of supervision of psychotherapy*. Paper presented at the Massachusetts Psychological Association Annual Meeting, Cambridge, MA.

Sadler, W. (1969). *Existence and love:* New York: Scribner.

Sartre, J. (1948a). *The emotions: Outline of a theory* (B. Frechtman, Trans.). New York: Philosophical Library.

Sartre, J. (1948b). *Anti-Semite and Jew* (G. Becker, Trans.). New York: Schocken. (Original work published 1946.)

Sartre, J. (1957). *Existentialism and human emotions* (H. Barnes and B. Frechtman, Trans.). New York: Philosophical Library.

Sass, L. (1987). Introspection, schizophrenia, and the fragmentation of self. *Representations, 19*, 1–34.

Sass, L. (in press). The truth-taking stare: A Heideggerian interpretation of a schizophrenic world. *Journal of Phenomenological Psychology*.

Schachtel, E. (1959). *Metamorphosis.* New York: Basic Books.

Schachtel, E. (1966). *Experiential foundations of Rorschach's test.* New York: Basic Books.

Schafer, R. (1948). *The clinical application of psychological tests: Diagnostic summaries and case studies.* New York: International Universities Press.

Schlesinger, A. (1986). *The cycles of American history.* Boston: Houghton Mifflin.

Schneider, K. (1984). Clients' perceptions of the positive and negative characteristics of their counselors. (Doctoral dissertation, Saybrook Institute, 1984). *Dissertation Abstracts International, 45*, (10), 3345B, 1985.

Schneider, K. (1986). Encountering and integrating Kierkegaard's absolute paradox. *Journal of Humanistic Psychology, 26*, (3), 62–80.

Schneider, K. (1987). The deified self: A "centaur" response to Wilber and the transpersonal movement. *Journal of Humanistic Psychology, 27*, (2), 196–216.

Schneider, K. (1989). Infallibility is so damn appealing: A reply to Ken Wilber. *Journal of Humanistic Psychology, 29* (4), 495–506.

Sechehaye, M. (1970). *Autobiography of a schizophrenic girl.* New York: New American Library.

Seligman, M. (1987, August, 29). Discussant. In R. Schwartz (Chair), *Cognitive-affective balance in anxiety, depression, and hypomania.* Symposium conducted at the annual convention of the American Psychological Association, New York City.

Selye, H. (1976). *The stress of life* (rev. ed.). New York: McGraw-Hill.

Shapiro, D. (1965). *Neurotic styles.* New York: Basic Books.

Smith, M., Glass, G., & Miller, T. (1980). *The benefits of psychotherapy.* Baltimore: Johns Hopkins University Press.

Solomon, R. (1981). *Love: Emotion, myth, and metaphor.* New York: Anchor/Doubleday.

Spiegelberg, H. (1976). *The phenomenological movement: A historical introduction* (Vols. 1 & 2). The Hague: Martinus Nijhoff.

Spinoza, B. (1955). *On the improvement of the understanding; The ethics; Correspondence* (R. Elwes, Trans.). New York: Dover. (Original work published in 1883.)

Spitz, R. (1965). *The first year of life.* New York: International Universities Press.

Stechler, G. & Kaplan, S. (1980). The development of the self: A psychoanalytic perspective. *The Psychoanalytic Study of the Child, 35,* 85–105.

Stechler, G. & Halton, A. (1987). The emergence of assertiveness and aggression during infancy: A psychoanalytic systems approach. *Journal of the American Psychoanalytic Association, 35* (4), 821–838.

Stein, D., Hardyck, J., & Smith, M. (1965). Race and belief: An open and shut case. *Journal of Personality and Social Psychology, 1,* 281–289.

Stevick, E. (1971). An empirical investigation of the experience of anger. In A. Giorgi, W.F. Fischer, & R. von Eckartsberg (Eds.), *Duquesne studies in phenomenological psychology* (Vol. 1, pp. 132–148). Pittsburgh: Duquesne University Press.

Strupp, H. (1978). Psychotherapy, research, and practice: An overview. In S. Garfield & A. Bergin (Eds.), *Handbook of psychotherapy research: An empirical analysis* (pp. 3–22). New York: Wiley.

Sullivan, H. (1953). *The interpersonal theory of psychiatry.* New York: Norton.

Sulloway, F. (1983). *Freud: Biologist of the mind.* New York: Basic Books.

Thomas, A., Chess, S., & Birch, H. (1968). *Temperament and behavior disorders in children.* New York: New York University Press.

Thomas, A. & Chess, S. (1977). *Temperament and development.* New York: Brunner/Mazel.

Thomas, A. & Chess, S. (1985). Genesis and evolution of behavioral disorders: From infancy to early adult life. In S. Chess & A. Thomas (Eds.), *Annual progress in child psychiatry and development* (pp. 140–158). New York: Brunner/Mazel.

Thoreau, H. (1961). *The heart of Thoreau's journals* (O. Shepard, Ed.). New York: Dover.

Tillich, P. (1952). *The courage to be*. New Haven, CT: Yale University Press.

Tillich, P. (1967). *My search for absolutes*. New York: Simon & Schuster.

Triandis, H. (1961). A note on Rokeach's theory of prejudice. *Journal of Abnormal and Social Psychology, 62*, 184–186.

Trotter, R. (1987, January). The play's the thing. *Psychology Today*, pp. 27–34.

Truax, C. Carkhuff, R., & Kodman, F. (1965). Relationships between therapist offered conditions and patient change in group psychotherapy. *Journal of Clinical Psychology, 21*, 327–329.

Tsanoff, R. (1949). *The ways of genius*. New York: Harper.

Vaillant, G. (1977) *Adaptation to life: How the best and the brightest came of age*. Boston: Little, Brown.

van den Berg, J. (1972). *A different existence: Principles of phenomenological psychopathology*. Pittsburgh: Duquesne University Press.

van Kaam, A. (1966). *Existential foundations of psychology.* Pittsburgh: Duquesne University Press.

Vonnegut, M. (1975). *The Eden express*. New York: Bantam.

Wagner, E. (1981). *The interpretation of projective test data: Theoretical and practical guidelines*. Springfield, IL: Charles C. Thomas.

Waite, R. (1971). Adolph Hitler's guilt feelings. *Journal of Interdisciplinary History 1*, (2), 229–249.

Webster's New World Dictionary (1968). *Webster's New World Dictionary of the American Language*. Cleveland: World Publishing Co.

Weick, K. (1984). Small wins: Redefining the scale of social problems. *American Psychologist, 39*, 40–49.

Wilber, K. (1981). Up from Eden: A transpersonal view of human evolution. Boulder, CO: Shambala.

Williams, R. (1984). The untrusting heart. *The Sciences, 24*, 31–36.

Wittgenstein, L. (1961). *Tractatus logico philosophicus* (D. Pears & B. McGuinness, Trans.). London: Routledge & Kegan Paul. (Original work published in 1921.)

Wolfe, B. (1988, April 23). *An integrated perspective on phobias*. Paper presented at the Society for the Exploration of Psychotherapy Integration, Cambridge, MA.

Wood, C. (1986, September). The hostile heart. *Psychology Today*, pp. 10–12.

Wrightsman, L. (1977). *Social Psychology* (2nd ed.). Monterey, CA: Brooks/Cole.

Yalom, I. (1980). *Existential psychotherapy.* New York: Basic Books.

Yerkes, R. & Dodson, J. (1908). The relation of strength of stimulus to rapidity of habit-formation. *Journal of Comparative Neurology, 18,* 459–482.

Zilbach, J. (1979). Family development and familial factors in etiology. In J. Noshpitz (Ed.), *Basic handbook of child psychiatry,* (Vol. 2, pp. 62–87). New York: Basic Books.

Zimbardo, P. (1977). *Shyness.* Reading, MA: Addison-Wesley.

INDEX

Abstraction, 23
Abstraction/concretization continuum, 30
Accidents, 39
Acute trauma
  case illustration of, 86–88
  developmental paradoxes, 76–79
Aggression
  expansion and, 39
  paradoxic understanding, 72
  psychoanalysis and, 61–62
Anarchy, 112
Anger, 67
Animals, 115–116
Anorexia nervosa, 46
Anti-Semitism, 107–110
Antisocial behavior, 49
Anxiety
  hyperconstriction and, 43–44
  physical health and, 154
Arousal mode, 31
Asserting, 30
Authoritarianism, 109
Authoritative parents, 169–170
Authority, 104
Autonomy, 43

Becker, Ernest, 7, 55, 173, 177, 183

Behavior, 22–23
Behavioral/cognitive psychology
  causality and, 58
  rapprochement and, 186
Bettelheim, Bruno, 141, 150
Bias. *See* Prejudice
Bigotry. *See* Prejudice
Biological mode (*umwelt*), 29*n*2
Birth
  existentialism and, 62
  psychoanalysis and, 61
Blake, William, 135
Body
  constriction and, 73
  See also Physical health
Borderline personality
  causation and, 95
  schizoid contrasted, 53–54
Borges, Jorge Luis, 17
Boundlessness, 66
Buber, Martin, 106, 165–166
Buddha, 179
Bugental, James, 201–202

Cancer, 154
Catastrophe
  constriction and, 74
  psychotomimetic drugs and, 70–71